Soccer is Fun
without Parents

Peter M. Jonas, Ph.D.

For information, contact
MSI Press
1760-F Airline Highway, #203
Hollister, CA 95023

Cover designed by Carl Leaver

Library of Congress Control Number 2019941941

ISBN: 978-1-933455-44-0

To: Elyse, Clara, Davis, Nina, and Ian

1. I love you
2. Good luck
3. Have fun

Peter M. Jonas, Ph.D.

Contents

Acknowledgements

A project this this typically takes the work of a team but in this case I did it all by myself, because I am that good. Not really, I need to acknowledge Denise Barnes who was not only my unofficial editor but kept my ego in balance, which is not easy to do. Jenna and Monica Story provided to be wonderful researchers and did a really professional job, despite having to work with me. A special thanks to Ian, Nina, Davis, Clara, and Elyse for their input on many of the stories. And last but not least, thank you Nancy for not divorcing me while I wrote this book. The problem is now you are stuck with me.

Peter M. Jonas, Ph.D.

Soccer is Fun without Parents

I never played soccer growing up but my son, Kevin, latched onto it about the same time he learned how to walk. I have learned how to love the sport by watching kids play and being a high school referee. Apparently, Americans don't find the sport exciting; not enough scoring, too many dives by players, slow action, etc. Have you ever watched a baseball game? Come on. Any NFL game typically entails only 11 minutes of actual playing time compared to 18 minutes in baseball, and 90 minutes in soccer. Despite what many Americans say about the sport, there is only one thing that needs to be fixed in soccer: parents.

When Kevin was about 12 years old, he tried out for a select team and made it. Little did my wife and I know that a select team means that you will only spend a "few" select nights and weekends at home. We travelled—a lot. Members of the FC (Football Club) lived in the greater Milwaukee area, but we travelled—every weekend it seemed like—to Chicago, the Midwest, outside the Midwest, the Dallas Cup, and any other tournaments with Cup in the title. FC was very successful, and the team won its fair share of games and tournaments, and of course, every parent assumed that their son would be getting a full ride to any college of their choosing. Not only does this not happen, but very few kids even get partial scholarships. Soccer does not exactly bring in the money that American football does. One time I made the mistake of calculating how much money I spent on soccer travel in one year, and let's just say that I paid for college several times over, so why was I worried about a scholarship?

We were thrilled when Kevin was selected for the FC team, and without much notice we were informed the team had a tournament that weekend. We travelled (of course) down to southern Illinois, about three hours away. It was great fun meeting all the kids and the parents—who I would spend more time with than my own wife over the next ten years. We arrived at the field for our first game of our first tournament. It was spring, so the temperatures had to be in the 40s with a brisk wind. Little did I know that I would spend most of my young adult life freezing, enduring the rain, and missing anything else of interest that transpired on a Saturday, because I was out on the "pitch." Maybe that is why parents are always yelling, they are just trying to stay warm.

I found a nice spot on the sidelines with my new friends. All the parents were huddled around one person, Tom, who appeared to be the leader of the group. He was collecting money, writing down information in a scratch pad and talking to everyone. I soon came to find out that he was taking bets on when (not if) a fellow parent, Bob, would be kicked out of the soccer match by the referee. Apparently Bob was a screamer, which you will read about later in this book. He loved to simply yell at the ref, yell at the coaches, yell at the players, and even yell at the other parents. Bob certainly did not let us down in the first game. Just after the start of the second half, Bob yelled out that his son was fouled with nothing called. "Come on ref, my son got sandwiched! You should know something about sandwiches." Let's just say that the referee was not a slender man and he did not take kindly to Bill's comment—which was simply one of hundreds already hurled at the officials throughout the match. The ref had had enough, and he came running over. To be honest, it was not even really a run. It was more of a waddle. Bob knew what was coming and wanted to get his money's worth. So, he screamed, "That is the fastest I have seen you run all day. Oh my gosh, it is a runaway bowling ball." Bob was then ceremoniously kicked out of the park as Tom quietly distributed money to the winner of the pool.

I soon came to realize that this was the norm. Parents certainly care about the game, but they care more about how their son, or daughter, is treated. There is certainly a wide-array of characteristics displayed by parents at soccer matches. Some are quiet as mice, some are very knowledgeable and simply admire the beautiful game, but too many are yellers, screamers, complainers, and simply out of line. This book focuses on the good, the bad, and mostly the ugly parents at soccer matches. People do not pay attention to boring information, so we will concentrate on the "non-boring" parent. I am not going to let you know which category I fit in, or how many categories I fit in. However, the moral of the story is that this book takes a humorous side of soccer (parents) and tries to identify the lifelong lessons that soccer can teach.

Research Design

I was a soccer dad for over 18 years and am still a high school soccer referee, going on my 20th year. I collected all of the stories in this book from personal experiences, interviews with fellow refs, and a survey distributed to soccer clubs all over the country. Occasionally, I included a story from the news that was just too good to pass up. I have always heard that truth is stranger than fiction but never imagined the accuracy of this expression.

Two years ago, I was the ref for my granddaughter's team. After the first ball went out of bounds, I yelled, "Pink's throw-in!" and I promptly heard my granddaughter, Elyse, say, "We are fuchsia, not pink." This is why I ref. Kids learn valuable lessons about life while playing soccer, and they have fun doing it. But mid-way through this U-6 game, one of the mothers started yelling at her daughter, who happened to be playing defense. She kept yelling, "Big kick!" "Big kick, Martha!" Of course, the team's coach was trying to teach control and possession. At one point I had to stop the match because someone needed to have their shoes tied. This is a very common occurrence in U-6 games, and the kids will not let you do it for them. They need to do it themselves, and it only take 10-15 minutes to accomplish this mundane task. At this time out, I went over to Martha and asked if that was her mother yelling. She sheepishly said, "Yes." I politely told Martha that her mother seems very nice, "but she is not giving you the best information. You should just listen to your coach and have fun." She smiled and said, "Thank You." Parents need to listen to their kids—and to the referees. This incident made me realize that parents are already starting their kids down the wrong path at age 5. What chance do the youth have by the time they are in high school?

The Matheny Manifesto

Mike Matheny is a former professional baseball catcher in America. He played 13 seasons in Major League Baseball (MLB) for the Milwaukee Brewers, Toronto Blue Jays, St. Louis Cardinals and San Francisco Giants. In addition to winning four Rawlings Gold Glove awards, he was a successful coach for seven years with the St. Cardinals. As a manager, his teams won on National League pennant and three central division titles. He knows what he is doing when it comes to baseball.

In 2008, a group of parents convinced Matheny to coach their little league team. Matheny had prepared for this day and once said, "I always said that the only team that I would coach would be a team of orphans, and now here we are." Matheny wrote about his experiences in his book, *The Matheny Manifesto: A Young Manager's Old-School Views on Success in Sports and Life*. Despite his reservation, Matheny decided to coach the little league team because he believed the biggest problem with youth sports had been the parents.

Before he coached even one practice, Matheny wrote a long and direct letter to all the parents. The letter, in part, read:

> My main goals are as follows: (1) to teach these young men how to play the game of baseball the right way, (2) to be a positive impact on them as young men, and (3) to do all of this with class. We may not win every game, but we will be the classiest coaches, players, and parents in every game we play. The boys are going to play with a respect for their teammates, opposition, and the umpires, no matter what.

> I believe that the biggest role of the parent is to be a silent source of encouragement. I think if you ask most boys what they would want their parents to do during the game, they would say, "NOTHING." Once again, this is ALL about the boys. I believe that a little league parent feels that they

must participate with loud cheering and, "Come on, let's go! You can do it!" which just adds more pressure to the kids.

These boys need to hear that you enjoyed watching them and you hope that they had fun. I know that it is going to be very hard not to coach from the stands and yell encouraging things to your son, but I am confident that this works in a negative way for their development and their enjoyment. Trust me on this. I am not saying that you cannot clap for your kids when they do well. I am saying that if you hand your child over to me to coach them, then let me do that job.

They will not shake their head, or pout, or say anything to the umpire. This is my job, and I will do it well. (Matheny, 2009)

Like soccer, Matheny knew that parents value the wrong things in the sport. Matheny knew that he needed to teach these young men how to play the game of baseball the right way, to be a positive impact on them as young men, and to teach teamwork, leadership, and emotional intelligence. Parents value wins, loses, and ERAs, which seems very ironic in a Twilight Zone sort of way.

Matheny had the right idea. Parents should be seen and not heard. Adults want to "discuss" the game with their kids on the ride home, but kids want distance after a match. They make a very rapid transition from athlete back to child, and they would prefer parents move just as quickly from spectator and "coach" to mom or dad.

Malcolm Gladwell, a bestselling author, noted that it takes approximately 10,000 hours to become an expert in an activity. Gladwell labeled this as the 10,000-Hour Rule, which he believes to be the key to success in any given task. The rule equates to 20 hours of work a week for 10 years. However, professor Anders Ericsson, a noted psychologist, disagreed with Gladwell writing that it takes 10,000 hours of "deliberate practice" to become an expert. What this means is that you need to fail and learn from your mistakes. Simply practicing 10,000 hours does not make you an expert, however, failing, reflecting, learning, and practicing can make you an expert.

What this means is that parents need to let their kids fail and learn from the experience. Athletics is one of the best ways for young people to take risks, make mistakes, and deal with failure without life and death consequences. The mistakes made on the soccer field do not stay on their permanent record. (I am not sure what a "permanent record" is, but according to my mother, mine is already filled to the point that they had to add an appendix.) We're talking about a game. Kids usually don't want, or need, a parent to rescue them when something goes wrong. Parents yelling from the sidelines only get in the way of their kids' learning.

A sad note in all of this is that approximately 75 percent of children who play organized sports quit by age 13. While there is no definitive answer about why, many researchers suggest that it is because of pressure from parents. A referee friend of mine always likes to say that he equates kid's soccer to a musical recital. Parents don't yell instructions to their seven-year old when they are singing or playing the piano. They are not jumping up from their seats when the proper chord is struck, yelling, "Great job Jimmy!" or "Big kick on the next chord!" Yet they feel it is OK to do so on the soccer field. Why?

Definitions

Before we move forward, we need to define a few terms. Part of the concern about parents yelling is that they do not know the rules of the game and are simply yelling the wrong information. Parents, if you are digging yourself into a hole, the least you can do is stop digging.

Soccer Terms:

- **Coach**: The focal point of abuse for parents, mainly because of playing time.

- **Hand ball:** When the hand hits the ball, not when the ball hits the hand. If you learn nothing else from this book, parents, please learn the offside rule and what is a hand ball.

- **ODP**: Olympic Development Program, or Only for Desperate Parents.

- **Off-side:** A rule not understood by parents, abused by players, the center of dispute by coaches and perfectly clear for refs.

- **Parent:** Can't have soccer players without them, but can't have good, fun soccer with them. In other words, we can't live with them and it is illegal to kill them.

- **Rec (Recreational Soccer)**: A level of soccer played by boys and girls solely for fun. Parents consider Rec soccer nothing more than purgatory before their child becomes a select player and then plays professionally.

- **Regionals:** A league developed by parents because they wanted to tell their friends that their children played teams from various neighboring states.

- **Select:** A soccer league that lies between Rec and ODP; another level of purgatory for parents.
- **Soccer Academy**: No one really knows the definition of a soccer academy, but parents love them all.
- **Soccer:** A game played by 11 boys or girls for the sole purpose of frustrating parents.
- **State Cup:** The ultimate soccer tournament played for the championship of the state and the ultimate bragging rights of parents.

Soccer Equipment for Parents

It is amazing to me that parents even attend soccer matches. It seems that all soccer games in the Midwest are played in very cold temperatures—far below normal—and can only be played in hail, stinging sheets of horizontal rain, and hurricane force winds. If you live in the south, the opposite is true. It must be 90 degrees with 90% humidity before any soccer match can start. Inclement weather and spilled coffee seem to be the only norms of the sport. I am not sure if the weather Gods hate soccer or if this is one way to get back at parents, who tend to use God's name in vain a lot at these matches. It is always interesting to see how parents adjust to the inclement weather. Bundling up in cold weather is an obvious solution, but some of the outfits parents wear are unbelievable.

In fact, the cost of some of the cold, hot, rain gear is outrageous. I could have included a section called the Fashion Parent in this book because there were people, like me, that did not care what they looked like, just so long as they stayed dry and warm. I purchased inventions that guaranteed to keep my hands and feet warm, devices to keep me dry, boots that were absolutely, positively waterproof (not!), portable fans for those hot days (that always seemed to fail), lights that helped us see for the night games (that always worked so much better on TV than in real life), and backpacks that contained straws that would supply liquid directly to my mouth with a simple push of a button. (I really thought that I needed this last one but realized using my hands worked better). I basically purchased enough equipment to start my own online store.

However, the chairs that parents carry with them are even more fun to ridicule. Every parent has a folding chair they carry with them. Most are slung over their shoulders like explorers moving through the Amazon in search of the fountain of youth. Some chairs are fancy, with cup holders, or umbrella holders, or the ability to seat three adults, much like a sofa in their living room. The greatest sitting utensil of all was owned by a woman. She brought a transparent "zipper house." I am not really sure how to describe it other than to say it was large enough for only one person sitting on one chair. It was completely transparent, so the person could see out all sides, but it was a mini-tent set up with four walls, four rods in each corner and zipped up on the side. This person merely set up her chair, "built" the plastic house around her, and zipped up to keep the cold and rain out and herself inside. It was sort of like bubble boy from the Seinfeld episodes meets soccer mom.

Game days are as much social events as they are sporting events. Parents are really attending the games to see their friends, to mingle, and to network. Sorry kids, but your parents need to get out of the house too, and soccer is merely an excuse to gossip with their neighbors. But it's not just a place for parents to get together—oh no. It's a place for them to chat, rage, speculate, fume, cheer, laugh, and more, all within the time-frame of an hour!

I am sure that you understand soccer is not only labeled as the beautiful sport, but it is played around the world. One of the "beauties" of the sport is that it can literally be played anywhere, anytime, and for very low cost. For example, in the poorest parts of the world, kids play football and all they need is an open space, something round to kick around, and two logs serving as goals. However, when the sport came to the United States, we almost immediately saw the emergence of The Soccer Mom. The popularity of the sport rose in the 1970s and '80s and was adopted mainly by the middle class in suburban America. Originally, soccer was safer than American football, more active than baseball, and had a certain European sophistication that enticed the bourgeoisie. Consequently, soccer was stereotyped as a white, suburban sport played by rich kids and run by the PTAs on grass—sometimes artificial grass, so our little loved ones don't get hurt or accumulate grass stains—god forbid.

To be part of the sport, parents also need to know about the following organizations.

> **AYSO**: (American Youth Soccer Organization) This is the bureaucratic arm of soccer that reminds us soccer is for winning, not for fun.

> **FIFA:** FIFA not only sets the rules for soccer but then promptly turns around to break all these rules through bribes, collusion, and corruption.

> **U.S. Club Soccer:** A National Association member of the U.S. Soccer Federation, U.S. Club Soccer is a non-profit organization committed to the development and support of soccer clubs in the United States.

U.S. Development Academy (U.S.DA): The U.S.DA is sort of like ODP but different. No one really knows how it is different, but like everything else, ODP and U.S.DA compete with each other for players and money.

The **United States Youth Soccer Association** (**U.S. Youth Soccer**) is the largest youth affiliate and member of U.S. Soccer, the governing body for soccer in the United States. If you are not confused yet by all the youth soccer organizations, you will be.

U.S.SF (United States Soccer Federation) The United States Soccer Federation (U.S.SF), commonly referred to as U.S. Soccer, is a 501(c)(3) nonprofit organization and the official governing body of the sport of soccer in the United States. No wonder parents are always yelling on the sidelines, they are just trying to figure out all the acronyms and myriad of organizations.

Soccer Rankings

No self-respecting parent discussed in this book is ignorant of the Youth Soccer Rankings U.S.A. This organization, and corresponding site, gives bragging rights to all parents from all walks of life. If your team is listed high enough in the rankings, you will be on top of the world, but lose a game and fall in the ranking and it is a disaster akin to losing half of your portfolio in the stock market. My guess is that most parents would rather lose 50% of their portfolio than fall below an arch-rival in the national youth soccer rankings. You never go to the soccer field without first checking the weather and your rankings at http://youthsoccerrankings.us or http://gotsoccer.com/rankings.aspx

You know you are a soccer family when ...

The following information is a compilation from a number of youth soccer associations:

- You have owned every style of camping chair ever made.

- You have never met a linesman that knows how to call off-sides properly.

- You have never met a competent Center Ref in your life.

- Your kid takes a bloody wallop on the nose, and your first thought is that he/she needs to quit crying because we're running out of time in the game.

- You know where every elementary school, middle school, high school, college, and park with a soccer field is in three different states, and you know where the closest Starbucks, bagel shop, and Subway is for each of those fields.

- You know how to get to all of the above without getting lost or consulting a GPS.

- Your gas credit card bills are bigger than your second mortgage.

- All of your vacation time is taken up by soccer events. No more beach vacations, unless your team gets invited to Surf Cup. No more ski vacations ever again!

- You know the closest grocery store to the practice fields because that is where you do your shopping.

- You have seen all kinds of movies between tournament games that you would have never watched otherwise.

- There are posters of Englishmen and Brazilians in your house.

- You've forgotten where you go to church.

- Your child's "good shoes" are his newest soccer cleats.

- You and your spouse spend all weekend driving to soccer games. In different cars...in different counties...with different kids. And talk on the cell phone only to compare scores. And don't see each other until Sunday night.

- You are happy to spend $140 on soccer cleats but are appalled when the materials for your child's science fair project cost $45.

- The kids on your team are "feisty," while the kids on the opposing team are "dirty."

- You have been to several cities in the country that have wonderful tourist attractions, but while in these cities you have seen only soccer fields, hotels, rental car counters, and airports.

- The mats on your car's rear floor are never free of dried grass and black turf pebbles.

- You, as soccer parents, have a strict rule about "no removing shin guards inside of the car."

- You look forward to Monday so that you can go back to work/school and relax.

- You have not celebrated your anniversary for three years because it always falls on a practice or game day.

- You own a two-year-old SUV with 182,000 original miles.

- You begin to use words like football, pitch, boots, sides, fixtures, and tables in a way that totally befuddles your non-soccer friends and family.

- Your closest friends are those that you've met through soccer.

- You can recognize most national team jerseys and the majority of major European club jerseys on sight.

- You go from an 8 to a 22 handicap in four years and you have not been invited to a golf scramble in the last two years because everyone knows you've got no game anymore!

- While watching the documentary "Supersize Me," you and the wife realize you have come close to duplicating that diet during consecutive weekends with tournaments.

- When you receive at least three copies of the "Eurosport" catalogue in the mail each week.

- When you wish you had bought stock in IGLOO because you own every shape and size of cooler and water bottle.

- When someone asks you how old your child is, you respond, "She's U-10."

- You drive home from the game complaining bitterly about the condition of the field and its adverse effect on your kid's game only to pull into your driveway and have your spouse point out the 14-inch high grass which has not been mowed in two weeks.

- You are up, driving to a game on a Saturday morning, it is raining, and Starbucks isn't even open yet.

- You have made no plans for any Labor Day or Memorial Day weekend, for years!

- You keep towels, newspapers, Febreze, lawn chairs, umbrellas, and water jugs in the trunk of ALL of your cars.

- You go to sell your car, the soccer ball magnet peels off the paint.

- You drive 80 miles for practice and think nothing of it.

- You get upset because teachers give assignments on practice nights. WHAT are they thinking?

- You spend $1,200 on a trip to San Diego for a tournament and don't even see the ocean.

- Your "favorite places" are all soccer related.

- You can sleep in a hotel room with 12 teenage boys all playing FIFA.

- Instead of buying a newspaper to read it...you get it to stuff your child's $120 cleats...

- You make your soccer trips into "family" vacations.

- You work your daughter's wedding in around your son's soccer tournaments.

- Your player holds up a yellow card when you and your spouse are arguing.

- You mourn your child's last year in high school because it will all be over, and you KNOW it was the best thing to happen to you and your kid. (Omega Athletic Club, 2007).

Outline of Chapters in Book: Servant Leadership

Now that you are officially a soccer family, the question is what type of soccer parent are you going to be? The following pages contain descriptions and examples of the various types of soccer parents. Let's just hope you do not see yourself in any of the descriptions. If this is true, you are either dead or your son is now out of college and no longer playing soccer. Each section starts with a general description of the category being described, followed by real-life examples from the soccer field—the pitch. You will also need to learn the lingo. For example, your kids wear boots, not shoes. It is the pitch, not a soccer field. Never call it a "hand ball" because it is "handling the ball," and of course, there are NO goalies—that is hockey. We have keepers. Keepers are the kids that love playing the position but whose parents hate it because they are the ones "scored on." Whenever anyone scores a goal, my wife says, "I feel so sorry for his mother."

At the end of each chapter is a resolution to make things better. Robert Greenleaf is the expert behind a theory entitled Servant Leadership. Greenleaf defines Servant Leadership this way: "The servant leader is servant first... It begins with the natural feeling that one wants to serve, to serve first." Traditional leadership models typically define leadership by position and are top-down power organizations. For example, the president is the leader, followed by the vice presidents and so on. However, the Servant Leader shares power, puts the needs of the employees first and helps people develop and perform as highly as possible.

This is what is missing in youth soccer. It is important to note that parents operate by the power pyramid model and need to follow the concepts of Servant Leadership. In fact, the great thing about this model is that youth soccer players are, in fact, learning the 12 principles of Servant Leadership simply by playing the sport. The parents, unfortunately, are operating under an old paradigm of top-down leadership. They are at the top, kids are right below, and refs are at the bottom of the food chain, to be devoured by sarcasm, spite, and rage. All for the stipend of about $30 a game.

Larry Spears (1995), CEO of the Greenleaf Center for Servant Leadership, defined the 12 Principles of Servant Leadership. The principles are listed below and will be highlighted at the end of each chapter to address the misguided actions of parents.

1. Listening
2. Empathy
3. Healing
4. Awareness
5. Persuasion
6. Conceptualization
7. Foresight
8. Stewardship
9. Growth
10. Building Community
11. Calling
12. Nurturing the Spirit - JOY!!

The Screamer (Parent)

The Screamer is loud, and you know them right away. They scream about the refs, the coaches, and most often, the players: "Get the ball!" "Big kick!" "Hustle Timmy, hustle!" Their voice typically carries into the next town, as if the louder they yell the better the kids play. It does not work that way, sorry. However, there is a direct correlation between how loud you yell and how embarrassed your kids are to be from the same family.

Have you ever thought about what the player thinks when parents are screaming at them? Here is someone twice as large as you, hollering at you all the time to perfectly complete tasks that you might not be skilled enough to perform. Talk about pressure! Freud would have a field day with the Screamer.

Sometimes it is not just one or two parents that do the unbelievable. Maybe the crowd mentality takes over and a group simply goes crazy. One beautiful day in Leyland, Texas a group of soccer parents used their mobile phones as a distraction for the goal tender (keeper) in a U-13 soccer match. Not just one or two crazy parents, but up to 100 supporters of Moston Brook under-13s, and rivals Knuzden of the Blackburn and Darwen District Junior League, were behind the goals at the Lancashire FA County Ground in Leyland for the Tesco-sponsored County Cup Final. Apparently the match was a draw, 2-2, and the game went to a penalty shoot-out, which Moston won. The incident started when the Moston Brook's 12-year-old goalkeeper, Alex, was sent off during the shoot-out for alleged comments made to the referee. Of course, this led to the Moston Brook manager, Michelle, and her assistant running onto the pitch to confront the referee. I think all soccer parents need to watch the Little League World series every year in Williamsport, PA. These kids have fun, play hard, and when they strike out, they smile and run back to the bench. The parents appear to cheer no matter what, and the umpires enjoy the game (Manchester Evening News, 2007).

Anyway, back to harsh reality. The match ended in controversy when parents cheered loudly after missed shots and flashed mobile phones at players to distract them during a penalty shoot-out. One official at the game said, "It was a disgraceful situation. The pair [manager and assistant manager] should not have come on the pitch, and the cheering of missed penalties and the use of mobile phones to put off young players taking penalties is frankly beyond belief." I guess in this electronic age anything is now possible (Manches Evening News, 2007).

Many countries are inflicted with the disease known as "soccer parents." The title of the following story tells it all: "Soccer Mom in Norway Attacks Player, Strangles Ref." The details of the incident are taken directly from the newspaper report in *Aftenposten*. A soccer mom took objection to a play on the field and decided to act. "A female parent from the visiting team came running onto the pitch and attacked a 13-year-old. She pushed the 13-year-old onto the ground, so the girl was lying on her back," Tor Eriksen of the Bardufoss regional sports association (BOIF) told NRK (Norwegian Broadcasting). The BOIF girls were called a range of nasty names and were also told to "get their ugly asses off the field." The excitable mother from Tromsø was not content with insults and flinging a girl to the ground. She then took a stranglehold on the referee and had to be restrained by BOIF leaders. Now *that* is parenting! And to think my mother only showed support for my team by bringing orange slices at halftime (The Fatref blogpost, 2007).

Not to be outdone, Deadspin reported the story of a mother who literally abandoned her 15-year-old on a highway. Apparently, the woman was disgusted with how the daughter played in a recent soccer match. On the ride home, the mother screamed at her 15-year-old daughter in the car about her performance and asked her to repeat areas of her game that needed improvement. When the daughter missed a few of the items, the mother slapped the daughter, ultimately getting so mad that she stopped along Interstate 80 and left her there. I am not sure what else to add to this story, but I think the daughter may be better on the road than with this mother.

Researchers Bruce Brown and Rob Miller asked college athletes what their parents said that made them feel great and brought them joy when they played sports. Trust me, none of the athletes said that being left on the side of the highway was how they learned the most from their parents. The most common response from the athletes was that they appreciated it most when their parents said, "I love to watch you play."

Many parents do, in fact, say they love to watch their little athletes play, but the problem is HOW they express this concept. The following is a story about a few parents who simply got too involved in a youth soccer match. Remember, this is youth soccer not the World Cup—but to be honest, it would be bad even at the World Cup. Two fathers, one from each opposing team, got into a "cheering" match. Granted, this was not a well refereed contest, but the referee was a young man in his late 20s trying his best. As the ref made one bad call after another, the parents egged him on. A bad call against the FC Clinton team meant that the parent from the FC Blast team would mock cheer, "Oh, great call, ref," and vice versa. This banter continued to escalate until most of the other parents were more annoyed with the two fathers than the poor referee. Let the shouting war begin. FC Clinton dad: "You cannot trip a player." FC Blast dad: "There was no tripping on the play. The girl is just clumsy," FC Clinton dad: "You cannot trip a player." FC Blast dad: "There was no tripping on the play. The girl is just clumsy." (Continue this cycle for a ridiculously long time and you get the idea.)

The referee should have just given his whistle to the two dads and let them finish reffing the game, but it was just at this point that the "cheering" got dreadful. FC Clinton dad: "Sit down and shut the hell up." FC Blast dad: "Why don't you just come over here and make me?" FC Clinton dad: "You are not worth the effort." FC Blast dad: "There will be no effort at all as I kick you're a$$." You must wonder how these two men hold normal jobs and have a family.

Thankfully, the wives of the two obnoxious, testosterone driven, narcissistic males intervened, and it did not come to blows. After the game, as the referee left the field and, of course, one of the "cheering" parents went up to give him a few comments, the ref was not having any of it. I heard him say, "I became a ref after a long career playing, and I know what I am doing. Besides, now that my playing days are over, if I can't enjoy the game, I'll make damn sure nobody else will." Drop the mic.

Here is advice for parents who consistently cheer, and jeer, their kids. It comes from R. Mendoza, who wrote on FUNdamental Soccer about "Coaching Children." Remember the following:

1. Parents spend the first two years of their life teaching kids to walk and talk. Then you spend the next sixteen years telling them to sit down and listen to your instructions.

2. Grandchildren are God's reward for not killing your own children.

4. Children seldom misquote you. In fact, they usually repeat word for word what you shouldn't have said.

5. The main purpose of holding children's parties is to remind yourself that there are children more awful than your own.

6. We childproofed our homes, but they are still getting in.

7. Be nice to your kids/players. They may choose or work in your nursing home one day.

And finally, if you have a lot of tension during soccer games, simply do what it says on the aspirin bottle. "Take two aspirin and keep away from children."

Rayvon is one of those Dr. Jekyll and Mr. Hype type of parents. At work or on the racquetball court, he is the nicest, most pleasant person. He doesn't argue with other players at racquetball, he is a servant leader at work, and everyone loves him. Rayvon even served in the military for many years, making rank of Sergeant. While serving in the military down south, his son played soccer on an elite team. Rayvon would get off duty and rush over to the pitch in his uniform to cheer on Robby. However, Rayvon's form of cheering may be a little different than what you are used to. He literally brought a megaphone to the games to yell at his son—which I am sure Robby thoroughly enjoyed (sarcasm). Rayvon would run up and down the sidelines, with his big megaphone, yelling "instructions" to Robby. The coaches disapproved of this action as much as Robby did, but to no avail. Then one day, the assistant coach simply walked over to Rayvon, took off his coaching jersey, handed it to Rayvon and walked away. You would think that he would be embarrassed, but instead, Rayvon did not miss a beat. He walked over next to the coach, megaphone still in hand, and continued his verbal diarrhea toward the players.

Rayvon should take note that on a military base in North Carolina, they place Marine Corps representatives around the field whose jobs are to note the final scores and make sure the youth soccer games run smoothly. One parent refers to them as "bouncers," for obvious reasons. My guess is that military parents at these games are very well behaved and do not get within six feet of the men who are in uniforms with guns. This is either a great idea or another sign of the apocalypse.

Some of the "quiet adults" fall into the category of overly cheering parents, too. These are the parents that sit in their folding chairs all game drinking coffee. You can spot them because they have coffee stains on all their shirts. This is because they sit and sit and sit until their team scores, and then they jump up (spilling their coffee) and cheer in an overexuberant way. They also get mad at those darn parents who never stop screaming from the sidelines, but the "quiet adults" are first to whisper to their neighbor when a team is doing poorly, and they love to spread rumors about what parent has a "special problem" or that one of the players from the other team is NOT eight years old. "Our coach needs to get a copy of his birth certificate because I know he is either nine or ten years old."

Another parent story recounts the adventures of Sandy, an elementary school counselor. Sandy was always willing to help and cheer on her "kids." She wanted all of them to get along and play together. One day during recess she noticed a girl standing by herself while all the other kids were playing soccer on the other side of the field. Sandy walked over to the young girl and asked if she was all right. The girl quietly said, "Yes." A little while later, however, Sandy noticed the girl was in the same spot, still by herself. Approaching again, Sandy offered, "Would you like me to be your friend?" The girl hesitated, then said, "Okay," looking at the woman suspiciously. Feeling she was making progress, Sandy then asked, "Why are you standing here all alone?" "Because," the little girl said with great exasperation, "I'm the goalie!"

If you have ever travelled to Muscatine, Iowa, you will find a small, quant village of about 22,000 people. Muscatine is on the Mississippi River but sort of in the middle of nowhere. Don't get me wrong, the city is nice but very rural. As you drive through town, you see small but well-kept homes, a local tavern, a quaint family grocery store, and a stop sign or two. Then you go up a steep hill and come out on the other side only to view the Field of Dreams. This is not really what it is called, but there is the Muscatine Soccer Complex, which is a 41-acre, $3.8 million soccer facility that features eight full-sized, state-of-the-art, premiere soccer fields. Two of the eight fields are internationally sized, lighted, and contain amended soils. The complex is fully equipped, including concessions, media centers, restroom facilities, and parking areas. It is the most beautiful grass you have ever seen in your life, in the middle of nowhere—again, sorry Muscatine. The complex sells t-shirts that say, "Badass Grass," and it is. I am including the story of Muscatine in this section of the book because when we first travelled to the field, a few of the parents kept saying, "If we can't win on this grass, we can't win anywhere." I thought to myself, *what does grass have to do with our team winning, and isn't the other team playing on the same grass?* I do have to admit that I was almost afraid to walk on the grass, in fear of hurting it or something. I laid down in the middle of the field just because it looked so comfortable. Sometimes parents act more like 8-year-olds than their real 8-year-old. During one game, the parents started a chant of, "Bad Ass Grass, Bad Ass Grass."

Servant Leadership: Listening

"Traditionally, leaders have been valued for their communication and decision-making skills. Servant-leaders must reinforce these important skills by making a deep commitment to listening intently to others. Servant-leaders seek to identify and clarify the will of a group. They seek to listen receptively to what is being done and said (not just said). Listening also encompasses getting in touch with one's inner voice and seeking to understand what is being communicated" (Spears, 1995, pp. 4-5).

Servant leaders listen. They do not listen to hear; they listen to understand. True servant leaders listen not only with their ears, but their eyes. Have you ever heard the expression, "actions speak louder than words?" Parents need to listen to coaches and their children, and then watch what they are doing. Moreover, communication involves what your kids say and what they do not say. Believe it or not, your kids are really smart. The leader/follower relationship is complex enough without parents yelling contradictory information to their children. Let your child develop soccer and leadership skills on the pitch.

It is ironic that we constantly ask our children to listen, but we do not really teach them how to do this. Stephen Covey, the author of *The 7 Habits of Highly Effective People*, identified five levels of listening:

1. Ignoring
2. Pretend listening
3. Selective listening
4. Attentive listening
5. Empathic listening

Really listening to people for understanding is level 5, and if parents would really practice empathic listening, they would learn that coaches and kids do not want them screaming at soccer matches. In addition, for a youth player to become good at soccer, he/she needs to really listen to their coaches to learn. Empathic listening is one skill learned in youth soccer.

Peter M. Jonas, Ph.D.

The Parent Who Wants to Be Coach

Parents want to be in charge. After all, this is what a parent is. They are in charge of clothes, in charge of transportation, in charge of discipline, etc., etc. When it comes to soccer, they also want to be in charge. The problem is, they have no idea how to coach or even what to coach. So, they delegate the responsibility to someone else, they pay exorbitant fees to be in the most prestigious soccer club, and then they proceed to "coach" from the sidelines. Little do these parents know, the real coach is trying to teach your child independence. The young players come in very dependent on the experienced coach, and hopefully they leave as independent players—that is the goal. The main challenge with this goal is the parent.

For example, one of the best stories about a parent-coach "wannabe" comes from a real coach in Tennessee who had a starting U-18 girl player. Brittany had quite a bit of talent, but occasionally she did things that she needed to learn from. The coach would simply pull her from the game, try to do a little instruction with her and maybe have her sit for a few minutes to reflect. However, Brittany's father almost consistently took this as a sign that he should "help out coaching." He literally left the stands and would sneak on to the bench and give his daughter more instructions. This happened a number of times at different games, to the point where the other parents started calling him the "undercover coach." The real coach tried to put an end to it, but Travis kept sneaking onto the bench. Finally, at the start of one game, Brittany slowly walked up into the stands and sat next to her father. Completely taken aback, Travis asked, "What are you doing here?" Brittany responded, "Coach said you wanted to sit by me, so this is the only place it is going to happen. I can only get back into the game if you promise not to come out of the stands." The parent got the message and all the other parents applauded when Brittany returned to the bench.

Coach Pete is a retired American soccer player who played professionally in the Major Indoor Soccer League, American Soccer League, United Soccer League, and American Indoor Soccer League. He coached at the professional, collegiate, and youth soccer level, where he is currently the coaching director. (This biographical data was taken from Wikipedia. Don't tell my students, but I love Wikipedia and use it all the time.) Pete said that, unfortunately, parents shouting instructions to youth soccer players throughout the game is the norm, but it is not helpful. Young boys and girls learning how to play the game need to make mistakes. They should not listen to parents who say, "Don't kick it to the middle of the field," or "Clear it." Parents want to win, but coaches want to coach. Young players need to learn how to make decisions for themselves, and when they lose the ball or kick it to an opponent, they learn a valuable lesson. The players will not learn much by constantly clearing the ball. They need to make mistakes in order to develop. Coach Pete said that he wants his players to work things out for themselves. More importantly, he wants players to explore new positions and not be cast into one spot on the field. This is how they learn the game, but vocal parents want their children to play one spot so the team can win. Coaches that listen to these parents put the more talented players in one position and never change them.

Unfortunately, the emphasis on winning and losing gets in the way of players growing, exploring, and having fun. Coach Pete said that he had a gifted player who showed real signs of becoming even better, but the parent moved his child off a U-10 team, even though they had won the state title, to another club where the new team had a better record. When asked about the decision, the parent indicated that the other team had a much better record, and therefore, the child would be happier playing for them. Really? Coaching is easy. You put a ball in front of a seven-year-old, establish goals, and let the players enjoy the sport. Create an environment that allows the players to be creative, to make mistakes, and to be themselves.

Bruce Reyes-Chow is a part-time blogger, consultant, and Presbyterian Teaching Elder, as well as a father to three soccer playing daughters. He writes that at one game for U-8 girls, the other team had at least "three parents or grandparents in some rotation standing behind their goalie, constantly in her ear telling her what to do, and at one time chastising the other defensive players for making X do it all by herself." The group of "coaches" were loud and proud. In addition, this team had five or so parents who had decided that the rules about who could be on the team side of the field did not apply to them. The other coach was clearly annoyed and politely said to one of the pretend coaches: "Excuse me, are you a coach? Only official coaches are supposed to be on this side of the field. Do you have your coach's card?" To which the opposing parent responded, "I'm not going to answer that." "Seriously?

Did you just plead the Fifth Amendment at an 8-year-old soccer game? I think this should be a clue that you might, just might, have crossed the line." However, self-regulation does not really work in the world of soccer (Words of Advice for Soccer Parents, 2011).

The Washington Area Girls Soccer League came up with at least a temporary solution to one group of parents who apparently all wanted to coach their team. In a preceding match, the parents could not keep quiet, trying to yell various instructions to their team and the referee. The league found that one father had raised his voice too loud and another parent displayed unusual "class" by yelling at the referee's daughter, "Your father should be fired!" I just wonder what the parent was thinking when yelling in front of the children that the father/coach should be fired for volunteering to coach a group of girl soccer players. There was a hearing by the league and they ruled that the parents for the Maryland team had to watch from 100 yards away for two games. Bravo for the Washington League and jeers to the parents who had to "sit in the corner" for acting like two-year olds.

The website *https://fundamentalsoccer.com/* ran a story on how parents love to scream and think they know how to coach. The website suggested that parents at a youth soccer match would make a great reality show. The idea is to take 10 of these soccer parents, have them coach youth soccer teams, and then slowly be eliminated. On this "show" the parent/coach would have to:

1. Win games and contend with screaming parent(s);
2. handle misconduct;
3. implement modern methods of coaching;
4. document attendance;

5. fill out game cards;

6. write a team newsletter;

7. compute progress;

8. keep parents informed;

9. play all kids equally—and win games;

10. complete evaluation reports;

11. communicate with parents;

12. arrange parent picnics and meetings;

13. give private lessons to those players who are behind;

14. strive to lighten the heavy players;

15. motivate the uninterested players;

16. find scholarships for the college bound players;

17. and make 'whole' the half players.

You get the idea. My guess is that everyone would be voted off the island within two days.

There is always one parent who has it all figured out. He/she knows all the players, how good they are, where they should play, yadda, yadda, yadda. These are the parents that will talk to other parents, unsolicited, and loudly run down the entire roster of who is good, who is bad, and who should not be on the team Of course, their own child is top of the list but is being underutilized by the coach. This parent even knows who is just taking up space on the roster and what player from a neighboring team should be on their team. Most parents do not pay attention to this type of talk because they are too busy looking for lost soccer balls and figuring out whose turn it is to bring snacks. By the way, these are two items kids worry about more than the soccer roster.

Recently, I was the ref for a middle school soccer match. I had worked at this school many times and liked the atmosphere because the parents are lowkey and the kids really are just having fun. In fact, the team could consist of 25 players or 11, depending on the level of homework that the teacher assigned that day or what was on TV. Anyway, I tend to be more lenient in these games because the players come with unmatched socks, different colored shorts, etc. In fact, the coach of the team did not really know soccer. On several occasions, I had to explain the rules to him, which seemed odd given that the school was paying him. Nevertheless, the kids on the team were great and they just wanted to play and have fun. However, this one day, a number of the players were not wearing socks or shin guards, so I politely informed the coach that, for player safety, these kids needed to be properly equipped. To my surprise, the coach nonchalantly said, "No, they don't. This is middle school and it doesn't matter." Seriously, it doesn't matter? Rules don't matter? Safety doesn't matter? My guess is that this individual was only the coach because a) he was being punished for something, or b) he was merely doing a side hustle from his normal job at the Jerk Store.

Servant Leadership: Empathy Servant

"Leaders strive to understand and empathize with others. People need to be accepted and recognized for their special and unique spirit. One must assume the good intentions of employees /partners and not reject them as people, even when forced to reject or call into question their behavior or performance" (Spears, 1995 p. 5).

As a parent, you should put yourself in the "boots" of the soccer player or the referee. How would you like it if an adult three times your age—your elder and your role model—was yelling obscenities at you? Swiss developmental psychologist Jean Piaget is one researcher who gives insight into the development of our youth. Piaget's theory of cognitive development suggests that children move through four different stages of mental development. The theory explains how children acquire knowledge, as well as understand information as they grow in aptitude. The bottom line is that youth are still developing physically, intellectually, and emotionally during their soccer-playing days. The behavior, or misbehavior, of adults during this time goes a long way in informing this development—both negatively and positively.

Soccer parents need to be more empathetic on the sidelines. How would you feel if you volunteered your time and expertise to coach a U-7 girls soccer team and the other parents shouted that you should be "fired?" My response would be, "Good. Fire me, and by the way, here is the whistle for you to take over." Youth soccer players learn empathy playing the game. They know that when a team mate scores an "own goal," they already feel bad. They will not rub it in because next time it might be them that makes the mistake. Moreover, the best coaches have played the game and know what the player is thinking and feeling. Unfortunately, many parents have not played soccer and instead respond to how *they* are feeling—not considering how the player is hearing the criticism from the sidelines.

Remember, Ambrose Bierce wrote, "Speak when you are angry and you will make the best speech you will ever regret."

Peter M. Jonas, Ph.D.

The Ego Parent

The ego parent is sometimes hard to spot at first. One key is that they are often seen with large insulated mugs of coffee that have some ridiculous inscription, like: "It is a great day for soccer." They also have bumper stickers about soccer on their cars, so you know they are involved with the "beautiful game." They will constantly bring up the premiership without really knowing what league it is or who plays in it, but they love saying the word premiership. The Brits put the emphasis on the first syllable of Premier, and Americans on the second. You know them within minutes of the conversation because their son or daughter, Sam or Julie, are the absolute best player on the team. There is no "we" in the Ego Parent.

In youth soccer there is a national ranking system where clubs, teams, and players get ranked. Too many parents take these rankings seriously, and the president of FC told a story that he had a parent from out of state call him because his family was possibly moving to Milwaukee. Ultimately, the family did not move because the father said that the FC U-12 girls' team wasn't ranked high enough in the country. The family currently lived in a city where the daughter's team was ranked really high, and therefore their club was a lot better. The father decided he couldn't be moving his daughter to play for an inferior team. Truth is stranger than fiction.

Don't for a minute think that fathers are the only parents with high egos. Jeff is a 20-year veteran referee who presented a player a Yellow Card for unsportsmanlike conduct. [Technically the term is unsporting behavior, not unsportsmanlike conduct.] The player was obviously removed from the game. However, just before Jeff was ready to restart play, the player's mother stepped on the field and started shouting at Jeff for giving her kid a card and at the coach for taking him out of the game. [The irony here is that with a yellow card the player *must* be removed from the game. This is the rule.] After several minutes of her rampage, the mother had to be escorted to the parking lot by the game manager. I am sure that she was later nominated for Mother of the Year for this display.

There is a rule of proportions in youth soccer. The better the youth player, the bigger of a jerk the parent is.

One team in Oregon tried to solve the problem of parents yelling by having shirts made for the coaches that read: "They play. I coach. You cheer."

One of the calmer soccer parents I know told this story to me because he believed it explained the Ego parent. (I am just repeating the story, not agreeing with the content.) Back in the Neanderthal times, the women worked by cooking the meals, bearing children, and building a cave/home that would help everyone survive. The men were the hunters and gatherers, going out in the woods. Soccer may not be that different. Soccer moms typically serve as team manager, handling all the paperwork, snack schedules, end of season parties, team communications, and more. They not only bear the children, but they also then drive them in a minivan that serves as the cave/home. The men gather intel on the opposing team players, and they hunt to coach and referee. If either of the two get out of line or create danger for the family, they pounce with every ounce of energy and soccer insult they can muster. At the end of the day, in either world, it is survival of the fittest. That especially rings true in select soccer.

Claudio Reyna, the Former U.S. Men's National Team World Cup Captain is credited with saying:

> For some reason, adults - some who can't even kick a ball - think it's perfectly okay to scream at children while they're playing soccer. How normal would it seem if a mother gave a six-year-old some crayons and a coloring book and started screaming? "Use the red crayon! Stay in the lines! Don't use yellow!" You think that child would develop a passion for drawing? Most important, parents must realize that playing sports is a way for children to express themselves (Reyna, 2008, para. 3).

There is a great Family Circus cartoon that depicts this thought. Billy is talking to Jimmy as they watch a professional soccer match. Billy says, "The reason they can play that good is because their parents aren't yelling at them from the sidelines." It is funny because it is true.

It is one thing to constantly yell at a youth soccer match, but negative behavior is raised to a whole new level when you yell profanities at a youth soccer ref, and you have definitely crossed a number of lines when you get kicked out of the soccer club and threatened with trespassing if you attend any more youth soccer matches. Thus, was the fate of Tinamarie Mahlum. The Thunder Mountain Soccer Association's board met to discuss this soccer mom and "held to verify continued complaints, slander, profanity, etc., against the League and board members." As a result, the league removed the entire family from any "membership activities of any kind with the Thunder Mountain Soccer Association." The director of the soccer league said that she was trying to act on behalf of children. She said, "Sometimes you just need to take the parents out of the sports." My point exactly! The child must have been thrilled with having to go to school the next day to face his friends after his mom's actions (Harmon, 2008).

Servant Leadership: Healing

"Learning to heal is a powerful force for transformation and integration. One of the great strengths of Servant Leadership is the potential for healing one's self and others. In, *The Servant as Leader*, Greenleaf writes, "There is something subtle communicated to those being served and led if, implicit in the compact between the servant-leader and led is the understanding that the search for wholeness is something that they have" (Spears, 1995, p.5).

Too many parents can't let go of the past, are worried about the future for their young soccer player, and certainly do not spend enough time in the present. They fear that a wrong call by the ref or move by the coach will forever hinder their child's soccer experience. More parents need to practice mindfulness. Mindfulness is the psychological process of bringing one's attention to experiences occurring in the present moment without judgement. It is being present to watch a soccer match, not think about the past or future, and calmly acknowledge and quietly accept one's feelings, thoughts, and sensations. The key here is "quietly." Research indicates that individuals spend 95% of their time worrying, or thinking, about the past or future and not enough time living in the present. Mindfulness also teaches us that all actions and thoughts are connected. When one parent yells, it is directly connected to the thoughts and actions of others. People need to live in Oneness. John Lennon simplified Oneness as, "I am he, as you are he, as you are me, and we are all together."

Peter M. Jonas, Ph.D.

The Passive-Aggressive Predator

The urban dictionary defines Passive-Aggressive as: "A defense mechanism that allows people who aren't comfortable being openly aggressive to get what they want under the guise of still trying to please others. They want their way, but they also want everyone to still like them" (Urban Dictionary, 2005). I merely added the noun of predator because it means: 1) an animal that naturally preys on others, "wolves are major predators of rodents," or 2) a person or group that ruthlessly exploits others. Both definitions fit in this case.

The more talented the soccer team, the more problems they have with parents. Many of the select soccer teams report that they have a plethora of families that simply don't pay to be in the club, and then come up with every excuse in the world not to pay their dues. It is typically the same families every year that say, "the check is in the mail," but the money never seems to arrive. This type of behavior puts the coaches in an extremely awkward situation and is without a doubt very passive-aggressive. One select team from Ohio found a solution. Before the start of an important tournament, the coach handed out letters to each of the players. They were told to give them to their parents and return immediately to the bench. The letters contained the amount overdue to the club. If the account was balanced, the note simply said, "Your account is fine, and your son will be playing as usual today." If the parents owed money, the letter simply read, "Your account is not in balance. You owe XYZ club $900, and your son will see the field when we see the money." Show me the money!

A lot of what goes on with the parents is basically some sort of clever manipulation. I hate to break this to you, but coaches see through this type of behavior. Parents are constantly coming up to coaches and saying things like, "All the parents are really wondering when you're going to start all the best players." In other words, "I'm wondering why my kid, who's obviously better than that other kid, isn't playing all the time." Passive-aggressive parents ask loads of questions like this. "Have you ever thought of this lineup? Have you ever thought of that lineup?" Of course, coaches try to do a good job of keeping those questions at bay. The other classic thing is for a parent to call a coach to ask about another player on the team. "I was just wondering if Jose is hurt because he just did not seem like himself today." One coach indicated that he gets calls like this all the time. Or parents calling about rumors regarding another player or something else happening without saying a name. Typically, this is done to get their own son or daughter more playing time. "You know, I think that Timmy, the U-10 player, is really a king pin drug trafficker and doing methamphetamine all the time. This is OK with me, but do you think he should be playing mid-field? Maybe he is better on the defense?"

During a rather physical tournament in Cincinnati, Ohio, several U-16 players got into a bench-clearing pushing match. No punches were thrown, but a parent-manager for the out-of-town team ran onto the field to "protect" his son.

(The key term here was PARENT-manager.) A player from the opposing team started yelling obscenities at the parent-manager, who promptly responded, "I am a devout Christian, G--d d---it, stop yelling your filthy mother-f------ obscenities at me!"

Most coaches say that they would rather have parents scream than be passive-aggressive in front of their children. At a Princeton youth soccer match (a small city in Wisconsin, not the University in New Jersey), the fans for one team were divided over their support of the current coach. Consequently, the two different sides sat by each other on the sidelines and spent the entire game shouting at each other instead of watching the game and supporting their kids.

In another instance, the parents were more united and decided collectively that they no longer supported the coach—even though he spent all his free time developing training plans, leading practice, sending out newsletters, meeting with kids after and before practice and so on. The parents would yell comments like, "Great job coach!" and, "Here comes the coach of the year!" in loud and sarcastic voices. Obviously, the coach and the kids could hear all this poor sportsmanship. However, on one occasion where the team was losing, the parents tossed insults about the coach's physical appearance and yelled a number (.237). It took a while, but the coach finally realized that this was his winning percentage for his U-13 girls.

Some youth organizations try to address negative behavior of parents by promoting Silent Games where parents are forbidden from talking during the soccer match. They can clap, but are forbidden from verbally cheering anything positive or negative. Now we are back to the concept that parents should be seen, but not heard, at soccer matches.

The National Association of Intercollegiate Athletics (NAIA) has also taken steps to address negative behavior. The NAIA developed a program entitled Champions of Character. The following is a pledge said before NAIA games by student-athletes:

> As a student-athlete, I pledge to accept the Champions of Character five core values. I will do my best to represent my team, my teammates and myself while striving to have the Integrity to know and do what is right; Respect my opponent, the officials, my teammates, my coach, myself and the game; take Responsibility by embracing opportunities to contribute; exemplify Sportsmanship by bringing my best to all competitions and provide Servant Leadership where I serve the common good while striving to be a personal and team leader. (NAIA website, no date)

Consequently, some youth organizations are following the same tactic by having athletes, as well as parents, sign behavioral contracts. (I guess this is what it has come down to.) For example, the Coastal Valley Soccer Club has Parent-Player contracts that state:

Parent/Fan Support

Parents/fans understand that once the game begins, their role is to support/encourage the athletes and the coaches. Parents/fans are not to interfere or undermine, in any way, the play of the game. Parents must refrain from "sideline" coaching. Essentially, parents are to refrain from speaking to the players during training sessions. Parents who act in an un-sportsmanlike manner or fail to abide by these rules risk having their child removed from the program by the coaching staff until the problem is corrected. Further action may be taken if necessary.

Parents must sign the contract where they agree to avoid nine different negative actions. Society used to worry about the athletes misbehaving, but now we must contract with the parents to make sure they are not misbehaving. I blame too much TV watching by adults.

Even the *New York Times* thought the topic was note-worthy when it published an article on May 28, 2006, entitled, "A New Cheer for Soccer Parents: Shush!" The Connecticut Junior Soccer Association conducts a Silent Sidelines weekend twice per year where parents are asked to "tone it down at games, to stop shouting directions from the sidelines, questioning a referee's call, or telling their children to hustle. The silent weekends, held the third weekend in May and the third weekend in October, first began in 2000. They were officially sanctioned in the junior soccer association guidelines in 2004."

One of the most interesting aspects of Silent Sidelines was that a young player requested the event because he, "wanted to play the game without being shouted at." I guess the expression is true, out of the mouths of babes comes true wisdom. Parents may not truly appreciate the gesture, but the majority of coaches love it because they believe that, "no instruction should be given to the players from the sidelines at any time and that no comments should ever be directed at the referee." Parents should come with instructions: "Warning, keep away from children."

So, leave it to the parents to screw up a good idea. A few of the adults interviewed for the *New York Times* article questioned the legality of the activity. They thought that it infringed on their freedom of speech. One parent noted that it sends the wrong message to the kids. He said, "That you have to keep everyone quiet for fear someone

Peter M. Jonas, Ph.D.

will say the wrong thing? That you can't trust the parents? I'm sure there are some parents who abuse it, but you don't have to go to the extreme." Youth organizations do need to go to this extreme, because one of the fundamental goals of soccer (pun intended) is for the players to work toward self-reliance, but parents think they must micromanage everything. How would parents like it if their kids went to work with them and yelled from the hallway, "Come on Dad, hustle at your job!" "Big kick and now go ask your boss for a raise!"

Silent Sidelines is not new, nor restricted to Connecticut. In El Paso, parents are required to complete a three-and-a-half-hour class on appropriate fan behavior. Parents must complete this course before their children can play in any city-sponsored youth sport. In Mission Viejo, California, a youth soccer league no longer records standings during the regular season for teams whose players are 8 to 11 years old. Unfortunately, several states have even had to approve (or are currently debating) bills that stiffen penalties for attacks on referees. Obviously, this action was the result of too many physical attacks on referees. Winning at all costs has taken on a new meaning.

In this day of video-taping everything, Brian Barlow, a youth soccer referee, has a Facebook page entitled, Offside, which he created out of frustration. He offers a $100 bounty for each video showing referee abuse by parents, in the hopes of shaming them to start acting more like humans. In 2001, a *New York Times* article reported that, "2,200 chapters of the National Alliance for Youth Sports show that about 15 percent of youth games involve some sort of verbal or physical abuse from parents or coaches, compared with 5 percent just five years ago." "According to a 2017 survey conducted by the National Association of Sports Officials, 87 percent of the 17,000 referee participants suffered verbal abuse in their role as officials. Thirteen percent said they had been subjected to a physical assault before, during, or after a game. That's almost one out of every seven officials claiming abuse of some sort" (Froh, 2018).

If it was not so sad, it would be funny, but the article was, of course, entitled: "New Rules for Soccer Parents: 1) No Yelling. 2) No Hitting Refs" (Wong, 2001).

Servant Leadership: Awareness

Larry Spears (1995) writes that, "general awareness, and especially self-awareness, strengthens the servant-leader. Making a commitment to foster awareness can be scary—one never knows what one may discover. Greenleaf observed—Awareness is not a giver of solace—it's just the opposite...Do others believe you have a strong awareness for what is going on? Servant leaders have a strong sense of what is going on around them. They are always looking for cues from their opinions and decisions. They know what's going on and will rarely be fooled" (Spears, 1995, p. 5).

In other words, kids, coaches, and spectators are aware when parents are being passive-aggressive. You are not fooling anyone. Once again, parents, take a lesson from your kids. They are out on the pitch learning how to be self-aware. Practicing how to learn from their mistakes and self-correct in the middle of a game. This skill happens to come in handy in all facets of life. There is a great scene from "The Office" where Michael asks Dwight, "What is the best advice I ever gave you?" Dwight responds, "Don't be an idiot. Whenever I am about to do something, I ask, 'Would an idiot do this?' and if the answer is, 'Yes,' I do not do that thing." The same advice goes to parents.

Peter M. Jonas, Ph.D.

The Pressure Parent

Anybody who coaches youth sports or volunteers in almost any youth sports organization, must accept that parents are part of the equation. Specifically, in youth soccer and in travel youth soccer—or elite youth soccer or whatever you want to call it—where parents pay coaches, coaches simply must understand that parents are going to want input. The education process isn't just about coaching kids, it's also about educating the parents about what you're trying to do, what you're trying to accomplish, and why you do the things you do. Youth soccer organizations need to coach soccer skills and life skills to both the youth and parents (e.g., educate the parents and have them embrace their enthusiasm and love for their own kids and the game). A Pressure Parent is one who applies pressure to the coach but does not work well under pressure—or under any circumstance.

A number of youth soccer associations have developed Parental Codes of Conduct. Many clubs have parents sign them as both an enforcement tool and an educational tool. One club included the following guidelines:

- I will never ridicule or yell at my child or another participant for making a mistake or losing a competition.

- I will respect the officials and their authority during matches and will never question, discuss, or confront coaches during a match, and will take time to speak with coaches at an agreed upon time and place.

- I will refrain from coaching my child or other players during matches, unless I am one of the official coaches of the team.

- I will never physically or verbally assault another parent, coach, official, player or volunteer.

No problem here right? Wrong! The club was officially notified by one of the parents, who of course was a lawyer, that the code was unlawful because it violated his constitutional right to free speech and if they proceeded to enforce the guideline, they would need to retain the services of an attorney and prepare for battle. So, this is what it has come to. My U-7 soccer player's lawyer is better than your lawyer. See you in court.

I have to include this next story in the section on the pressure parent because it involves a three year old and her father. It came from a great website labeled http://crassparenting.com, but the site appears to no longer exist. Too bad, it had a great name going for it. I guess you are just going to have to believe me on this one. Much of this story is taken directly from the website. Kids are starting to play soccer at younger ages each year. Micro soccer is probably just one way for soccer clubs to make more money and have more parents join, so why not? A young mother enrolled her three-year-old to play soccer. In this case, play really meant sit on the grass and watch as the ball rolled by, if it actually did roll at any time. There was another young three-year-old on the team named Lucy, who was actually in her second year of soccer. (Do the math, 3-1 =2. Seriously, there is a league for two-year olds?) Lucy's dad would probably fit into many of the chapters in this book, the Screaming Parent, the Win at All Costs Parent, etc. During one game, he really found his voice, yelling:

- "Dammit Lucy, I showed up to see you PLAY!!"
- "Lucy, you're not focused!"
- "Lucy, you are running around aimlessly!"
- "Dammit Sheila (or whatever his wife's name is), she's not even trying!"

Lucy was talented, but it may not take much athleticism to steal a ball from a three-year-old who is picking dandelions on the field, or one who is crying because he wants ice cream. Now when I say that Lucy was talented, it just means that she knew the ball was round and would roll if you hit it. The game continued until Lucy's team won after she scored a Kajillion goals. I often wonder what happened to Lucy. The coach indicated that she moved on to a more rigorous team, but I can guarantee her father is still there screaming out instructions. My guess is that to find Lucy, just follow the noise of her father yelling at a tee ball umpire or soccer ref. "I just hope she doesn't end up graduating first in her rehab class."

One day I want to see a seven-year-old respond to a screaming parent who is pressuring her on the sidelines. In other words, I want a team of seven-year-old soccer players to stop in the middle of a game and start yelling instructions to their parents. "Get up out of the chair and move around." "You are doing it all wrong! Work together as a group! Pass the lemonade! NO, not in the middle of the field! Big kick, parents!" At one soccer match, a coach yelled to his six-year- old player to "give him a target on the flank." "Excuse me! Give him a target on the what? Do you realize I'm six years old? How little time do you spend with six-year-olds that would make you think 'Give him a target on the flank' makes any sense to us? Maybe after we learn how to kick the ball farther than five yards we can start giving each other targets on the whatever" (Woitalla, 2007). It's true. Kids know that they are supposed to "Pass it," "Pass it," "Pass it," but sometimes they just want to "Dribble it," "Dribble it," "Dribble it." This is how they learn.

Paul Coughlin writes in his blog that as a coach he has dealt with parent complaints, but for him, mothers seem to be the worst. Coughlin has labels for his "protective" mothers. First there are the "'Helicopter Moms,' who hover above their children in a near-constant state of anxiety; 'Momma Bears,' those who are highly protective of their children and don't care if they disparage others in the process; and 'Grizzly Moms,' a highly dangerous breed who seem unwilling to stop at anything in getting their child what they want" (Coughlin, 2008). Be careful parents, because Coughlin believes that if your son or daughter is a "bubble" player, they may not make the team if there is a Momma Bear behind them. "Most coaches are volunteers. Why should they keep your kid and put up with you?"

However, Robyn wrote an article on her blog entitled, "Soccer Moms from Hell" (June 22, 2008), that not all moms are created equal. In fact, even though most youth soccer organizations depend on every parent volunteering or helping in some way, there are some parents who don't care. They "just want to drop off their kids at practice, let someone else watch them, and pick them up after practice. These same parents, of course, will be the first to complain when they don't like something." Why can't everyone just be like me, the "Perfect Parent"?

Servant Leadership: Persuasion Servant

"Leaders rely on persuasion, rather than positional authority in making decisions. Servant-leaders seek to convince others, rather than coerce compliance. This particular element offers one of the clearest distinctions between the traditional authoritarian model and that of Servant Leadership. The servant-leader is effective at building consensus within groups (Spears, 1995, pp. 5-6).

Remember: "You catch more flies with honey than vinegar," or, "Be nice. And if you can't do that, just don't be mean," by Richelle E. Goodrich; or, "It's nice to be important, but it's more important to be nice," by Author Unknown; or, "Be nice to people on your way up because you'll meet them on your way down," by Wilson Mizner.

Peter M. Jonas, Ph.D.

The Blame Parent

In many instances, the coach is also a parent. This is a deadly combination. Listed below are some of the short quips that refs have told me they use when the coach gets out of control—in other words, almost every game.

- Coach, if you have an assistant, you should warm him up.

- Coach, say one more word and someone is leaving. Since I haven't been paid yet, it won't be me.

- Coach, I am not stopping the game to talk to you now. We can do this later when we have dinner tonight.

- Stop yelling, I get enough of that at home. I came here for the peace and quiet.

- I always carry an extra whistle, so that when someone yells, I just show them the whistle and ask them if they want it.

- When parents yell "That was a hand ball!" you say, "No, that was a ball hand."

- There is a notoriously hot-headed coach in a local suburb. One ref went up before a game and said,

"Do you want a red card now or should I wait for the game to start?"

During a game in Michigan, a high school player twisted an ankle. The ref promptly called for the trainer to come out. Within seconds the trainer said, "Turn around, you won't believe this." A mother in a cocktail dress and stilettos was running onto the field. She pushed the ref out of the way and ran to her son. I heard her say, "I told you to be careful—you know what's going to happen to that $86,000 scholarship." The son replied, "Ref, please help me and call her off. I don't know who this woman is." The mother was furious at her son, but she did leave. The ref recounted the sight of this mother trying to storm off the field as her high heels dug into the soft ground making it almost impossible to even walk.

Unfortunately, fights on the pitch often occur in soccer matches, but when they spill over into the stands, it is another level. On a rainy night in New Jersey a U-14 match got out of control when two players got into a shoving match that escalated into a fight. Unfortunately, the game was being refereed by a parent because the certified ref did not show. Nevertheless, the Downtown United boys were playing the Brooklyn Italians under the lights on a Wednesday evening at Pier 40 when the incident started. Once the soccer players got into the skirmish, the parents decided to "help out." It became a chaotic situation, with one parent eventually being arrested and charged with third-degree assault by the Sixth Police Precinct.

It should come as no surprise that almost every witness had a different version of how the fight started. Some blamed the players, most blamed the parents, and some even blamed the fact that no official referee was on the field. One parent said that, "This would never have happened with a good referee," shaking his head. So, it is bad enough that the parents started throwing punches, but many of the adults said that the responsible party for the fight was a poor referee sitting at home because he forgot about the match and lost out on his $25 fee. It is bad enough to be arrested for assault at a U-14 soccer match, but it is almost funny when you place blame on an absent 16-year-old who was at home playing video games (Stiles, 2005). I am sure this parent truly loves teamwork, because it helps to put the blame on someone else.

Referee Jeff related a story from when he was the center official for a U-14 game. Just after a goal had been scored, a parent yelled out, "That was your fault Jimmy. If you had been doing your job, they would not have scored." Without missing a beat, the player stopped dead in his tracks and yelled back, "Shut the hell up, Ma!" While laughing under his breath, Jeff had to card the young man for unsportsmanlike conduct. His coach then pulled Jimmy from the game, which was probably a good idea. Just before the coach was to put Jimmy back in the game, his mother stepped on the field and started to shout at the ref for giving her kid a card, and then turned her ire onto the coach for taking him out of the game. After several minutes of her rampage, she had to be escorted to the parking lot by the game manager. Interestingly, Jimmy seemed to take it all in stride and subsequently re-entered the game and played without incident.

If you are a soccer parent, you know that there is a plethora of national youth tournaments played every year. Teams desperately work for the privilege of playing in tournaments, such as, the Best of the Midwest, the Dallas Cup, SAC United Premier - Columbus Day, and even the Disney Cup International Youth Soccer Tournament. Pachuca FC from Miami played against the Orlando EC/QPR Academy at the Disney Cup one year. Most of these tournaments are comprised of select teams, with bragging rights at stake and sometimes potential college scholarships. The level of competition also raises the excitement level, as well as the anxiety level. Such was the case when the Miami team lost 2 to 1 to the Orlando team. However, instead of handshakes after the game, there were kicks and punches. Some of the players in the match were involved in the free-for-all, but Jesus Albornoz said, "[He] comes to me and punches me and scratches me in the face, and I punch him, and I said, 'Don't touch me!'" Jesus ended up with a swollen eye and scratch on his face. However, the punch did not come "from a rival teenaged soccer player, but from a parent on the other team. The reason for the violence on the field is unclear but it has turned into a blame game." I always say, to err is human but to blame someone else shows real potential for political office.

The result is that the Osceola County Sheriff's Office is recommending that the player be charged with felony battery. Blame for the incident spreads far and wide, as the Orlando team accused parents of the Miami players of storming the field and hurting their kids. The kicker in the whole story is that, "A grandparent was punched in the chest, and his pacemaker went off." I am not really sure what it means that the pacemaker went off, but this cannot be good (Avalos, 2013).

Nobody gets blamed for things more than the poor soccer referee. I am a 60-something adult male with a doctorate. I lived through raising three teenagers, have five grandkids, and have been teaching for almost 40 years, and yet I can barely handle the criticism that sometimes gets thrown at me by parents. Once you reach 55, you sort of stop caring about what other people think about you and just live your life, so maybe the key to being a good referee is to get old and lose your hearing. Frank Monaldo recounts the following joke in a blog entitled, "The Role of a Soccer Referee." There is an apocryphal story about three soccer referees discussing the different ways they officiate games. In humility, the first referee says that he calls them as he sees them. Reflecting a little more confidence, the second referee says he calls them as they are. Possessed of even more epistemological certitude, the third referee claims that they are not anything until he calls them (Frank's Case Book, 2002). Basically, the referee is a baby sitter for the adults who is responsible for the safety on the pitch and who will get blamed for "bad" calls. You have to remember that at least 50% of the parents think that every call is "bad." A referee's job is to help mold the character of our youth and then to be able to tell parents to "go to hell so well that they look forward to the journey."

Servant Leadership: Conceptualization Servant

"Leaders seek to nurture their abilities to 'dream great dreams.' They have the ability to look at the organization, and any issues within the organization, from a conceptualizing perspective. This means the leader must think beyond day-to-day realities. Servant leaders must seek a delicate balance between conceptualization and day-to-day focus" (Spears, 1995, p. 6).

One of the most significant concerns for soccer coaches is that when parents scream or blame others for "problems," it teaches the young soccer player to do the same. Wayne Gretzky was asked how he became such a great hockey player, and he said, "I don't skate to where the puck is, I skate to where it is going." This type of conceptualization is fundamental in sports. To steal a few clichés, this is when the game slows down for the athletes and they get in a zone. This cannot happen when parents are bellowing at their kids—they need to learn these skills after many mistakes and learning for themselves.

Seriously?

This section is simply called Seriously? because I have no other words for the actions of some parents. I am sure that other stories may also fit into this chapter, but it is interesting how some parents seriously do the strangest things when it comes to sports.

In one soccer tournament in Illinois, a young player received a red card. The next day, he was back on the field. Of course, that's illegal and he should not have been allowed to play, but he did, and the coach of that team was hoping no one would catch him breaking a rule—seriously, you need to blatantly break rules in a U-13 soccer match? A parent from the opposing team from the prior day showed up at the game to make sure that kid wasn't playing. Seriously, Dad #2, you have nothing better to do but show up the next day at a game that has nothing to do with your son to watch what other adults are doing? Well, the young man was in the lineup and so, of course, the parent got into a fist fight with the opposing coach over that kid's eligibility to play.

If that is not bad enough, in that very same tournament, a field marshal got into a fist fight with the referee. The field marshal, of course, was a volunteer parent helping run the tournament who didn't like the way the ref was calling the game. As you know, the field marshal is supposed to be representing the tournament and keeping peace. Instead he was disrupting the tournament because he felt his team was getting slighted by the referee. So, two fist-fights in one weekend. Standard youth soccer tournament stuff.

A number of periodicals have run short stories on signs that "the Apocalypse" is here when it comes to soccer. *Sports Illustrated* may have provided some of the best fodder on this topic. Of course, all of these stories involve adults:

1. A mob of Argentine soccer fans hijacked two city buses at knifepoint to get to a match in Buenos Aires on time.

2. Two men got into a fight at a soccer match. One of the wives yelled out, "Be easy on my husband, he has a bad heart."

3. Johnny Jones, amateur soccer player in Newark, Delaware, was arrested after allegedly biting a referee on the chin. The police there are really taking a bite out of crime.

4. One coach yelled out to a ref, complaining that a player was always off-side. The ref, attempting to be clever, politely explained that he was not off-side. He simply was a skilled player and could move faster than the coach could see. The coach retorted, "If he is a skilled player, then I am a priest."

5. Referee Tom had his car keyed after a game. Several parents followed him to the car and keyed it as he drove off. The worst part was the police officer who watched and laughed.

6. Referee Kim recounted that he carded a player for calling his own teammate a "f--ker." When the ref went over to explain this to the coach, the coach said, "Well he is a f--ker."

7. Referee Wayne carries a large flashlight and a night stick. He keeps it in plain sight as he walks to his car after a game, so parents think he is a police officer.

8. A parent followed a ref to his car after a game that ended 1-0. The parent yelled, "How dare you call a PK with one minute left in the game!" The ref simply stared at the parent and pointed to his own chest. "What is under your shirt?" the man said. The ref replied, "An honest man."

9. Referee Ron was known for talking to coaches during a game. For example, one day he said, "Coach, number six is about to watch the game from the bench. You may want to sub him now."

10. Referee Jeff carries two sets of cards with him in a game because once a parent ran onto the field, grabbed his yellow and red cards out of his hand, and threw them into the crowd.

11. During the game, a parent put up his hands in a "fight" position, yelling to the ref, "Want to dance?" Ref yelled back, "You're not my type."

12. Referee Mark would never kick a parent out of a game. He would simply call the parent over at half time or at a major break and explain that once the center turns his back, the parent was to leave quietly, thereby saving the dignity of all.

13. Listed below are notes that have been left on cars of referees:

- Die!

- You suck worse than my teacher

- If we had instant replay, you would see how bad you are

- You suck, you suck, now off to ref you f___

14. A girl had in an earring prior to the start of a match. The ref told her to take it out, but the mother came out of the stands to say no because it was a starter earring and needed to stay in. They agreed to sign a waiver and let her play. Of course, within ten minutes the women took a header and started bleeding. The mother yelled at the ref.

15. In the middle of the game, an AR noticed a man slowly walk out of the stands and across the track and then sit on the bench of the visiting team. When there was a break in the action, the AR asked the man what he was doing. The man replied that his son needed a few lessons and the coach was "screwing up the game," so he had to come down to explain what needed to be done.

The Milwaukee Journal-Sentinel *reported in 2008 that:*

An off-duty Waukesha police officer and another Waukesha man got into an altercation at their daughters' soccer game, forcing the referees to stop the game and other parents to call 911 for crowd control. Both men have been referred to the Waukesha County District Attorney for a possible charge of disorderly conduct.

Apparently, during the game there was a series of bickering and name calling, escalating to more heated exchanges. The game was played between nine and 10 year old girls.

The 911 call indicated that two men were "acting like children."

According to reports, the off-duty police officer was heard yelling "get in front of her and slap her if you need to. Just slap her."

That prompted the mother of another child to say that the comment was not appropriate. The off-duty police officer called her out and said she should say that to his face.

Just then, the wife of the off-duty police officer arrived and was told what happened. The officer indicated that he got into it with the first lady.

The Waukesha man who overheard the comment called the officer a vulgar name. The two ended up chest-to-chest exchanging vulgarities. Punches were thrown at which point the game was stopped until the men left the park. They did leave but the incident escalated in the parking lot with more alleged punches thrown and the one man running over the foot of the officer with a car. So, without the parents, the soccer match resumed.

Soccer parents can surprise you both on the pitch, at the sidelines, and even in the office. Volunteers run most youth soccer organizations. A volunteer is a dedicated person who believes in "all work and no pay." Except for the following. There must be an entire level of hell in Dante's Inferno dedicated to those shameless individuals who steal from the youth. Seriously, why not just go into the piggy bank of an 11-year-old and take her nickels and dimes? Nevertheless, the *Athletic Business Journal* reported in 2013 that the Terrace Brier Soccer Club almost had to cancel its fall season because the treasurer issued 106 checks to herself, depleting all the resources. The Director of the Orange

Recreational League of Massachusetts allegedly used more than $45,000 of club funds for private purchases, including a down payment on a Humvee. (Really, you can't at least get an electric car and help the environment?) In Montgomery County, a soccer mom went to court to face charges that she stole more than $70,000 from a youth sports organization. The prosecutor summed it up nicely; "She was supposed to teach kids right from wrong, instead she showed them how to embezzle." Obviously, these individuals thought that CFO meant Chief Fraud Office.

On another note, one soccer match was just about ready to start when five women from one of the teams made an entrance onto the sidelines. They were all dressed in black sweaters with shiny gold and silver accoutrements surrounding a large picture of their sons on the soccer team. I know it is the job of parents to embarrass their kids, but even I felt sorry for these eight-year old boys. To make matters worse, on the back of the sweaters the women had placed the number of their young player, along with the number of goals and assists thus far in the season. I just wonder what they do after the next game, do they keep changing it? Seriously?

Servant Leadership: Foresight

"Foresight is a characteristic that enables servant-leaders to understand lessons from the past, the realities of the present, and the likely consequence of a decision in the future. It is deeply rooted in the intuitive mind" (Spears, 1995).

This entire book is basically a lesson in foresight. We need to learn from the past and realize that not all parents are created equal. In order to plan for the future, the first lesson probably needs to be that parents will do really dumb things. How can soccer organizations teach youth soccer by affording opportunities to develop servant leadership without parents messing it up? The last sentence is written "tongue-in-cheek," because youth soccer groups need parents and kids need parents. Youth soccer needs to figure out a way to develop parents as well as the young soccer player. Woody Allen had a great one liner about foresight. He said that he knew everyone was going to die someday, including himself, but he just did not want to be around when it happened.

Peter M. Jonas, Ph.D.

The Poor Sport

The Poor Sport is not someone who feels sad about losing, they are the parents that feel bad about losing and then do something about it. It is not the feeling that is a concern, but the actions that follow. You have to understand that the brain is wired for competition. Millions of years ago, the brain developed with one goal in mind—stay alive. Consequently, competition is an innate trait within the brain that is connected to survival. When a sabre tooth tiger attacks a group of cave men/women, you do not have to be the fastest runner, you just can't be the slowest. When you invite competition in youth soccer, it sharpens the mind for the player, but apparently triggers the wrong part of the amygdala for the parent. The amygdala controls the fight or flight decision. Soccer players respond by fighting through the adversity—working harder. Parents respond by fighting. Again, how ironic that kids learn while parents burn.

One story may exemplify the Poor Sport parent. At one point during a game, the coach called one of his seven-year-old soccer players aside and asked, "Do you understand what cooperation is? What a team is?" The little boy nodded in the affirmative.

"Do you understand that what matters is whether we win or lose together as a team?" The little boy nodded yes.

"So," the coach continued, "I'm sure you know, when a foul is called, you shouldn't argue, curse, attack the referee, or call him a pecker-head. Do you understand all that?" Again, the little boy nodded.

He continued, "And when I take you out of the game so another boy gets a chance to play, it's not good sportsmanship to call your coach 'a dumb nitwit' is it?" Again, the little boy nodded.

"Good," said the coach. "Now go over there and explain all that to your parents."

The story above is really a joke, but in real life one referee, Mitch, told me a story from when he went to watch his grandsons play in a large youth soccer tournament. One of the officials didn't show up, so the tournament organizers, knowing that Mitch was a referee, asked him to officiate a U-8 game. The opponents were not at all evenly matched. One team was very good and everyone on the team had advanced skills. For the little guys on the other team, the ball was square. Only one player seemed to know how to play. Because they were so young and so mismatched, the game probably appeared very ugly, with the final score being 21-0. As Mitch left the field, a mother from the losing team ran after him. She was very angry and told Mitch that she was going to report him because Mitch so obviously favored the other team, and she thought it was a shame that this tournament didn't provide "real" referees. Mitch is a 25 year veteran, this was a U-8 game, the score was 21-0, and Mitch's grandson was on the losing team. This is the ultimate definition of a poor sport. Moreover, I am pretty sure the ref had little to do with 21 goals being scored.

One parent took matters into her own hands after a similar lopsided score in a soccer match. She decided to write a letter to the parents of the winning team. Here is the letter she penned.

Dear Winning Team Parents,

Congratulations! Your 7-year-old boys beat our 7-year-old boys, although "beat" seems like a weak term for what just happened, dontcha think? It's probably more appropriate to say that your team pulverized us. Left us for dead. Wrung us out and hung us up to dry. It was brutal for us to watch, and you probably won't be surprised when I tell you that this kind of thing has happened to our boys before.

You could call our team the Bad News Bears of the local soccer league—our players are total noobs and they bumble and fumble and stumble their way through each and every game. They're learning new skills every week and giving it their best effort and they're definitely improving—but that's hard to tell when they play a team like yours, filled with kids who've been playing soccer together for years, practicing twice a week, attending soccer camps and clinics, and receiving hours upon hours of meticulous one-on-one instruction from their personal trainer (otherwise known as Dad).

With that kind of effort, you *totally* deserve to win—but there are a few things you could do to make it a little easier on us, The Losers.

Moms, we all love to cheer our kids on, but when you're up by 10 or more goals, perhaps it's time for you to shut the hell up. I'm sure you mean well (on second thought, I'm not so sure about that at all), but when you're sitting next to me shrieking about how amazing little Farkington is after his fifth hat trick, it's all I can do not to fold up my camp chair and shove it in your pie-hole. It's time for some #realtalk, my friend: The fact that your kid can score repeatedly in a rec league against kids who are new to soccer does **not mean** that he's the next Clint Dempsey.

Aw, did I just crush your hopes and dreams? Sorry.

Winning Team Coach (or should I say coaches, since every dad on your team is standing behind you, telling you what to do?), is it *necessary* for your little guys to win this game 35 to nothing? I mean, do you get a free personal pan pizza for that or something? Because you sure do seem to enjoy it. I guess the utterly dejected faces of our little boys just add to your pleasure. Glad that decimating 7-year-olds makes your day, dude. I'm sure it'll make for some great memories when you head back to your cubicle on Monday.

Oh, don't get your jerseys in a wad—I'm just kidding with you. Still, after 14 years spent on the youth soccer sidelines, I can tell you with confidence that I'm just giving you a souped-up version of what all the parents on the losing side are *thinking*. I've been on your side, too, Winning Team, more times than I can count, and I don't fault you for yelling your heart out when the game is a close one and the teams are evenly matched.

But if you don't know this already, let me clue you in: when you're up by five or more, shouting out how many goals your kid has scored each time he does, it gets annoying for the parents on the other team. So does watching the coaches and dads loudly high-five and back slap across the field when the score reaches 20-to-nothing.

Yes, we're all adults and ultimately, we can take it. But what *really* makes your behavior inexcusable is the fact that your kids now think it's appropriate. I can tell you without hesitation that if my child did a *victory dance* after scoring the 15th goal against a team that was woefully outmatched, I'd be out on that field in a hot second, leading him off it by the ear. But I got to watch your boys do this repeatedly last weekend as you all clapped and shouted encouragement and gave them big indulgent grins.

Seriously, parents? This shit *matters*.

One year from today, this soccer season will be a distant memory. Five years down the road, no one will remember the final scores, or who made each goal, or even the names of most of the boys on the team.

What will remain with these kids, what will become *ingrained* within them, is how they played the game. And I don't care what you tell your children about sportsmanship—if you're not living it yourself from the sidelines, it doesn't mean anything.

That's all. See you next weekend.

Sincerely,

A Mom from the Losing Team

(http://www.huffingtonpost.com/lindsay-ferrier/notes-from-the-losing-team_b_5939548.html?utm_hp_ref=tw)

Servant Leadership: Stewardship

Larry Spears (1995) writes that "Servant Leaders are often characterized by a strong sense of stewardship. Stewardship stems from medieval times when a steward would be assigned to hone the skills and development of the young prince to prepare him for his reign. A steward in an organization is responsible for preparing it for its destiny, usually for the betterment of society. When we describe a leader as having a strong sense of stewardship, we refer to a desire to prepare the organization to contribute to the greater good of society—not unlike preparing the prince to serve the greater good of the kingdom" (Rockwood Preparatory Academy, n.d., para. 8).

Being a poor sport does NOT contribute to the greater good of society. In fact, parents on the winning team need to practice stewardship. Parents are entrusted to not only take care of their children, but to instill strong values, and rubbing in a lopsided victory is not good stewardship. Unfortunately, too many parents turn to doing the right thing after everything else fails. However, the kids playing the game typically do learn and practice stewardship. They learn to respect the game of soccer and realize that the integrity of the game is more important than winning or losing.

This analogy may better explain stewardship: A man died and went to heaven. He is at the Pearly Gates by St. Peter, who led him down the golden streets. They walked by mansions after beautiful estates until they came to the end of the road where they stopped in front of a little shack. The man asked St. Peter why he got a simple hut when there were so many mansions where he would be more comfortable. St. Peter replied, "I did the best with the money you sent us."

The Parent Who Is Always Wrong

OK, here is the thing. Every parent who yells should probably be given a set of rules to read. Parents, you cannot just make up rules and yell them at me. As a referee I laugh every time someone yells, "That's a foul, high kick," or, "come on ref, call it both ways." First, there is no rule against a "high kick." Now, there are rules relating to playing in a dangerous manner, but there is no language about a high kick. Perfectly legal. Secondly, whether you know this or not, as a ref I do not care one bit who wins or loses the match I am officiating. Every call, 50% of the people are yelling at me, and I do not care if the blue team or red team parents are yelling. It is all the same to me. I do not play favorites, because I could absolutely care less who wins. I have no secret grudge against any eight-year-old player or its team.

Do not get me started on the off-side rule. Parents, players can be in the off side position and NOT be off side. The rule is pretty straight forward. I know it. All the refs know it. The kids know it. Parents, you should learn it. The rule reads that:

> A player in an offside position is only penalized
> if, at the moment the ball touches or is played by

one of his team, he is, in the opinion of the referee, involved in active play by:

- interfering with play, or

- interfering with an opponent, or

- gaining an advantage by being in that position

The key here is, IN THE OPINION OF THE REFEREE. Guess what, I am always right, because it is my opinion and despite what you may think, I am NOT going to change my mind. Do you think that the more you yell at me, the more I am going to give the advantage to your team, seriously?

There are a plethora of rules that parents simply do not understand, so if this is the case, why are you yelling? You want me to enforce a non-existent rule. For example, the ENTIRE ball needs to be outside of the touch line to be out, not one-half of the ball, or three-quarters—ALL of it. A handball—really this is handling the ball—involves a deliberate act of a player contacting the ball with his hand or arm. The referee must take the following into consideration:

- the movement of the hand towards the ball (not the ball towards the hand)

- the distance between the opponent and the ball (unexpected ball)

- the position of the hand does not necessarily mean that there is an infringement

In other words, if the ball hits a player's hand, it is not automatically a "hand ball." There needs to be deliberate action on the part of the player. Let me recap: 1) There is no such thing as a handball, but there is handling the ball. 2) When the ball hits the hand accidentally, it is not handling the ball. The opposite may be accurate for quidditch, but we are playing soccer.

I know this is hard to believe, but your kids know what they are doing. I hate to break this to you, but youth soccer is not about winning, it is about teamwork, collaboration, learning the basics of the game, and cooperation. Not everyone's child can, or should, play forward. One of the most cited criticisms of coaches is that, according to the parent, the child is playing out of position. There is no such thing as having 10 forwards on the field. Someone must play mid-field, defense, and be a keeper.

Here is a real-life story about a "know-it-all" parent. There was a U-13 girls' team that won Regionals and were moving onto the National Championship. Typically, every state has a State Cup tournament in soccer by age group. If a team wins State Cup, they move on to Regionals, and if they win Regionals, they move on to the National Championship. Despite winning Regionals—which is certainly a significant accomplishment—one parent was not at all happy. Martha was a member of the team and was pressed into playing keeper (goalie) because of an injury to the original keeper. Almost immediately following the celebration of winning Regionals, Martha's father on the FC team got into the coach's face and called him every name in the book—and none of them were compliments. Apparently, he was furious that his daughter was "stuck" playing goalie and she, of course, was a "natural" striker. This team eventually made it to the final four in the country, before losing to the eventual national champion, but the team did this without Martha. Her father pulled Martha from the team over this dispute and thus deprived her of celebrating with her team mates. By the way, celebrating achievements is a key component to developing a learning community and Servant Leadership. Parents need to learn this.

Because I am an educator, I feel as though I need to teach parents what to say and what not to say. First, my best advice is, "A closed mouth gathers no feet." If you do have to speak, think about this fact: Research indicates that men say about 5,000 words each day but only 400-500 really have meaning.

Here is a list of expressions that parents have yelled to refs over the years. If you see anything that you have said, my advice is stop right now and re-think your life:

- "If you had glasses, you would have caught that one." Please, at least be original.

- One parent told the Assistant Referee to stop stepping in front of her because she could not see her son and she "came to see my son play, not you."

- "Come on ref, call it both ways!" There are several responses to this. First, we can only call it both ways. There are only two teams. Second, do you honestly think that we only call it one way just to piss you off? That, somehow, we spotted you in the crowd and decided as a group, "Yah, that guy right there. Let's make sure that we make every call against that one gentleman."

- Parents say, "Great call ref." Then 10 seconds later it's, "Terrible call, you idiot." How could I become such an idiot in 10 seconds? I suppose it's possible.

- "That is NOT a foul, he hit the ball first." Let me just say that if the player hits the ball first and then commits murder, it is still second degree homicide. Hitting the ball does not take away the fact that one player kicked the leg of the other player and fouled him. Deal with it.

- "You finally got one right, ref. They have been doing it all game." First, thanks for the verbal acknowledgement that I got one right. Appreciate the vote of confidence. If they really have been doing this particular action all game, I probably would have noticed. But again, thanks for bringing this to my attention.

- "I'm blind, I'm deaf, I wanna be a ref!" Again, can we at least be original? The reality is that I am old and being deaf is not bad, at least I cannot hear the ridiculous comments from parents.

- "Come on, even Stevie Wonder saw that one!" I must assume that this suggestion violates ADA of 1990 somehow.

- One referee said to me that he heard the following from a group of parents: "Oscar Mayer, Oscar Mayer, that's bologna." Wow, I cannot even image an adult that thinks this is clever. I would bet this individual cannot spell bologna.

The following insults have been hurdled at a ref at some time. I must admit, when I heard a few of them I smiled inside. Nevertheless, they still demonstrate inaccurate information on the part of parents.

- "Hey ref, you might want to check your voicemail, YOU'VE MISSED A FEW CALLS!"

- "Come on, people have gotten pregnant from less contact than that."

- One time, after several parents were done yelling at me, another fan said: "NICE CALL, DAD!"

- "I've gotten better calls from my ex-wife!"

- It ain't Christmas yet, quit giving em' presents!

You may think that your comment is original, funny, or clever, but they really make refs sort of feel sorry for you.

Just as an important side note, there are two main categories of laws in soccer: Fouls and Misconduct. Parents need to learn the difference between the two. The following conditions must be met for an offense to be considered a foul:

1. it must be committed by a player

2. it must occur on the field of play

3. it must occur while the ball is in play

Remove any one of these conditions and the offense is not and cannot be a foul. Fouls can only occur when the ball is in play, but misconduct can occur when it's out of play as well. By the way, if you think you know the rules, you are wrong. If you think you don't know the rules, you are right. I would rather have you right than wrong, so let's just always go with the latter.

It is not just on the pitch that parents have inaccurate views of football or bellow outdated expressions. It is all over the United States. First, only seven percent of Americans view soccer as their favorite sport, and the majority of adults have the wrong impression of the sport. For example, an athlete asked one local high school gym teacher why soccer was not part of the physical education curriculum. His response was that soccer had a "direct link to communism." This teacher would turn red in the face and almost lose all bodily functions when discussing that "un-American, does-not-even-use-hands, non-sport." To him, soccer was a plot to destroy American values, developed by the likes of Marx and Lenin. This may have been a tad bit of an over-reaction. You must think about this one...

soccer was invented by communists to take over America! It is no wonder that people worry about the American education system.

There should also be a category for the "weather parent." You know, the one who is always looking at his phone and telling everyone what the weather is going to be. "It is going to rain in 31 minutes, and we are never going to get this soccer game in." This "weather parent" is always wrong, but even when they are not, they are always annoying. I am not sure why the older we get the more concerned with the weather we get, but it happens. One coach told me that parents are very excited when they enroll their child to play youth soccer, but very soon they are praying for rain to cancel practice or the game.

Servant Leadership: Growth

"Do employees believe that you are committed to helping them develop and grow? Servant leaders have a strong commitment to the growth of people. They believe that all employees have something to offer beyond their tangible contributions. Servant leaders work hard to help employees develop in a number of ways. Servant-leaders need to connect to others' developmental needs and actively find ways to help them reach their true potential as employees" (Rockwood Preparatory Academy, n.d., para. 9).

Youth playing soccer need to learn how to win and how to lose. They need to experience both sides of the coin to grow from the experience. One of the great benefits of soccer is that youth grow from being very dependent players to independent young adults. We can only hope that parents grow too. That is, grow out of yelling immature comments like, "Nuts and bolts, we got screwed" (this is seriously something parents say), to simply telling their kids,

"I love you and I hope you had fun," and that one referee named Peter Jonas is certainly worth his weight in gold.

Win at all Costs Parent

Win at all Costs Parents are diabolical. They just think differently than the normal adult. Of course, I am not sure what "normal" is in the youth soccer world. They will surreptitiously walk into the opponent's group of parents to see what they can hear. As if the head coach of the opposing team has handouts of their game plan to distribute to the parents and maybe, just maybe, the Win at all Costs Parent can find one handout laying on the ground. This parent also completes reconnaissance on opposing players. "Johnny cannot go left," or, "The keeper just got a D on his last history paper, so he is vulnerable." This group of parents also uses whatever means necessary to "recruit" the best players from other teams, and interestingly are self-proclaimed weather experts. They think they know what teams play better in the heat or rain and are constantly monitoring the Weather Channel for any change in the climate. This skill does come in handy when severe weather is about to hit, you just need to put up with the, "I told you so," comments.

Many years ago, a coach told me this story. In the middle of a U-18 boy's game, a player from the home team kicked the "star" player from the other team. The young man received a yellow card, but not a red card, and was able to continue playing in the game. Unbeknownst to everyone else, the father of the player that was kicked went to his car and got a gun. He took it into the stands, explaining to people sitting next to him that he was going to show the player who kicked his son "a real red card." Fortunately, someone called the police and the man was arrested.

The story does not end here. The player who kicked the man's son grew up to be an indoor soccer player who received some fame. He eventually became the head of a local soccer club. One day, the son of the gun-wielding man became a member of the same local soccer club. The head of the club approached the father, twenty years after the gun incident. The coach simply went up to the father and said, "You owe me an apology." Without hesitation or asking for more information, the man responded, "I am truly sorry for my actions."

Winning is so important to parents that they seem to lose sight of their values and family norms. Rebecca Thatcher was an investigative reporter who decided to try her hand at coaching. Her experience ended with her writing an article entitled, "Drug Smugglers vs. Soccer Parents," where she claimed she was more afraid of the latter than the former.

The problem is not only an over emphasis on winning, with the associated screaming and complaining, but the manner in which most parents respond to losing. Even the most lucratively paid soccer professionals talk about how the game needs to be fun. I am pretty sure your nine-year-old should feel the same way.

The quest for victories may be reality for all parents, but it especially rings true for Win at All Costs parents—they love taking pictures of their son and/or daughter. First, I think some mothers have their kids join soccer just because they look so cute in those uniforms. No matter where an Win atAll Costs parent goes, the camera will follow. They not only take picture after picture of their kids, forgetting about the rest of the team, but they record every game and post everything on social media. Of course, they only follow their own offspring throughout the game, so you have no idea what is really happening, e.g., the team could be winning or losing. The Facebook page of these parents is filled with pictures of their little super star on the field at a multiplicity of venues. My reaction is that if parents are on Facebook—get off now and never return. Secondly, most people do not even know that little Jimmy had a sister. All they see are pictures of Jimmy in his cute uniform with no pictures or even mention that he has a sibling. I am sure these young ladies will grow up well adjusted. Or maybe not.

Take, for example, the story of Bobby, who was a talented soccer player. If you do not believe me, just ask his mother. In fact, you do not have to ask her, because Linda will flat out tell you this information without you even mentioning soccer FC Groverton and FC Cumberland were the two strongest clubs at the U-12 level and they each won State Cup a number of years. Bobby played for FC Cumberland at U-12, which had a great team, but one year, they lost State Cup to FC Groverton. Linda was not happy and transferred Bobby over to FC Groverton for U-13. Now you may have seen this coming, but FC Cumberland won State Cup the next year for the U-13 boys. You guessed it, Bobby transferred back to FC Cumberland for the U-14 team. Now, I may not have to write this, but FC Groverton won State Cup the following year.

The kids just wanted to play the sport, so each year he was accepted back onto the different teams. Parents are another matter. While talking with Linda, the parents, from both teams, were accepting, professional, and kind.

Behind her back, Linda was the second coming of Beelze-bub. You "gotta" love parents who want to win at all costs.

Maybe the problem here is that every stakeholder has a different set of goals. The kids are trying to have fun and be with friends. Coaches want to develop their players. Parents want to win. In England, academy teams play non-competitive soccer up until U-16 or U-17. All matches are "friendlies" with no league standings. England has set the goal of player development at the top of its list and thus has dictated the soccer environment, which is not results ori-entated. It takes time, effort, and practice to truly develop into a soccer coach.

The coach needs to have communication skills, teach-ing skills, a sense of humor, planning skills, evaluation skills, practical skills, etc. Unfortunately, in many cities across the United States, a father or mother takes on the role of coach because, "no one else can find the time to do it," or because they have kids on the team. This dream job can turn into a nightmare when the other parents become experts after watching only a few games. I often equate this situation to teaching. I spent 10 years in college and gradu-ate school to learn how to teach, and I think on some days I may actually do a good job. Yet, some students who "went" to school seem to think they are experts in teaching be-cause they sat in a classroom. It is the same thing with soc-cer. Coaches spend years learning their craft and getting licensed, yet parents watch one match and they are experts and willing to tell a coach "how it really needs to be done." It is funny that all parents have their own set of opinions, which is fine. The problem comes in when all the parents have their own set of facts.

Of course, not all coaches are created equal. We all need to respect the work of each coach, but one soccer player from FC tells the story of a coach who was a perfectionist. One day during an unusually bad practice, the coach became disgruntled, pulling out the star player and saying that he, "did not seem to be hustling." The coach then instructed the player to run down to the river, find a piece of grass and bring it back to him in a hurry. The young soccer player responded immediately, but when he returned, coach yelled, "Wrong one."

Servant Leadership: Building Community

"Do employees feel a strong sense of community? Servant leaders have a strong sense of community spirit and work hard to foster it in an organization. They believe the organization needs to function as a community and work hard to build community within. Servant-leaders are aware that the shift from local communities to large institutions as the primary shaper of humanity has changed our perceptions and caused a sense of loss. Servant-leaders seek to identify a means for building community among those who are part of the organization" (Rockwood Preparatory Academy, n.d., para. 10).

Developing a sense of community entails trust, strong relationships, and a common, shared vision. It also means agreement on a set of values. When the coach is trying to teach, players are trying to learn, but parents are trying to win. This is not a community. What do you call a parent in a Learning Community? A visitor. Trust is the most important concept that parents need to embrace when it comes to soccer and coaches. There is an expression that, "it is better to trust the man who is frequently in error, than one who is never in doubt." Another key aspect of a community is that mistakes will be made (by everyone) and people can, and should, learn from them. "Anyone who has never made a mistake, has never tried anything new."

Peter M. Jonas, Ph.D.

The Never Stop Talking Parent

The Never Stop Talking Parent is also the one who must dissect every play and offer ideas on how to improve to anyone standing in talking distance. They always have a game plan that is better than the coaches, and even if they are horribly wrong about a predication or comment, it never phases them—they just keep talking.

One game, when I was the Center Referee, I had a parent who would not stop talking very loudly on the sidelines. Unfortunately, he was in the first row and called his son by name and number. I felt sorry for Mikael #7, and at one point in the game, I was next to this forward and I told him that if his father kept yelling dissent from the stands, I was going to have to eject him. The boy was devastated. This was a high school match and the thought of having his father publicly shamed was the worst form of punishment. Mikael asked if he could take care of it. I was not sure what he was going to do, but I said yes and waited with anticipation for his next move. Mikael asked his coach to be subbed, and then he surreptitiously walked over to the stands, whispered to his father and came back into the game. At the end of the match, I asked #7 what he said to his father, and he simply smiled and said, "If you keep yelling the ref is going to eject you, and if that happens, I am going to leave soccer and join choir."

Sara is a coach for a young soccer league and she wants to "coach" parents as much as her players. Sara will pull a U-8 player from a game if the parent is yelling—anything. The child then needs to walk over to the parent and say, "I was pulled out because you were yelling and can go back in if you promise not to yell anymore."

I am not sure if this story is true or not, but it certainly reflects the theme of the day: parents yelling.

Coach: "So what is your favorite position?"

Player: "Center Midfield."

Coach: "Interesting. Is that because you see yourself as a good playmaker and stopper?"

Player: "No, its because my dad is on one side and my coach is on the other, and sometimes if I'm in midfield, I can't hear either of them."

Just in case you do not know this, coaches would prefer parents not attend practice. Coaches need the players to pay attention to them and not their mother or father. One coach had a parent who constantly bellowed at her son because he kept laughing in practice. Are you kidding me! Research indicates that laughing is not only good for you, but kids laugh 10 times more than adults. You know why we decrease laughter as an adult? Because American culture shames us into it. We are told not to laugh at work, that "this"—whatever "this" is—must be taken seriously. Yet, laughter decreases stress, it builds relationships, and improves the culture of the team. Plus, individuals with a sense of humor live 8-10 years longer than those who do not. So, please parents, please let your kids laugh at practice. In fact, kids, laugh in the game and laugh on the car ride home when your parents seem to constantly relive the game. How many parents does it take to change a light bulb? 10,001. One to do the work and 10,000 reminiscing about every aspect of how great the old light bulb was.

Coach Pratt recalls one parent on his team that simply had to talk throughout a match. The players were told to ignore Mr. Davidson, but he was constantly spouting information, instructions, and sometimes just nonsense. "Go to goal!" "Watch number 4, watch number 4! Seriously, watch number 4!" "Shoot, shoot, shoot!" "Run faster, faster, faster!" "Be the ball, Jimmy"—what the heck does this mean? "No, don't shoot, what are you doing? Oh, OK, great shot." Of course, Mr. Davidson could not help but yell instructions, "Sammy go left, go right, now dribble more, take the space, cross it now, look for Malik out right, pass left, go forward." The funny thing is that most of the kids said they could not hear Mr. Davidson, and his own son said, "I cannot hear my dad at all, but when I do, I just ignore him at the game—just like I do at home."

One FC Grafton coach, Bryon, said that it typically is not one parent who will not stop talking. Over the weeks, it is the nonsensical, unrelenting blabber of everyone. As a coach you get to hear what parents thought about the game, the kids, and how they played. In addition, you learn what parents think about the coaches, how the refs did their jobs, what the parents from the other team thought about all of the above and what the parents on our team thought about the behavior of the parents from the other team. How are kids supposed to make sense out of all this noise? It is no wonder they get confused. Everyone is talking and telling them what to do. One game, Bryon decided to not say a word. Not just about coaching, but about everything during the game. He gave the lineup to his U-14 boys and said, "Play hard, communicate, and have fun," and that was it for the next 80 minutes. Parents were confused, the refs smiled the entire game, and the kids probably had the most fun they could have. After the match, the players and coaches reflected on the game and then were told to go home, forget about soccer, and just have fun—which they did.

I fully understand the interest of parents in watching their child play soccer, but one very wise parent tweeted: "When choosing a sport for your child, always consider the availability of indoor plumbing before deciding where to invest your money" (Maddox, 2015).

Some of the worst sideline parents are what is known as the ego-driven parent. They never stop talking about their kids. Moreover, they typically have low emotional intelligence and take it very personally when anyone criticizes their children, especially during a game. They have an emotional meltdown with any decision that is whistled against their child, any foul called, or a pass that should have gone to their future star and instead it didn't arrive or went to someone else. They especially hate it when a free-kick or a corner is taken by someone else. These are all situations when the ego-parent goes nuts and vents their anger.

Young soccer players are cute. Take, for example, little Elyse who was playing a game one beautiful Saturday afternoon when she saw one parent with a camera. Elyse noticed this parent, left her position on the pitch (instead of chasing the ball), ran over to the photographer and posed for photos. While this soccer-player model-to-be was posing, the parent turned photographer started yelling, "Get back on the field and play your position!" Let's stop and think about this. You take an expensive camera and point it at an eight-year-old and you DON'T think they are going to pose for you? Then you keep taking pictures and expect them to concentrate on soccer and not the camera? Seriously, who is the delusional one here—the parent or the eight-year-old? How many quiet soccer parents does it take to change a light bulb? It hasn't been done yet, because we can't find one.

Soccer referees can make anywhere between $10 and $55 per game. One ten-year-old excitedly explained that, "I like the money. Sometimes you get $25 for an hour of work." These kids are reffing because they love the game, they love their fellow football players, and they love the money. Show me the money. So, when an adult, who knows only a fraction of the rules, yells at a ref, they are slowly chipping away at their innocence and that "love of the game."

Obviously, for adults, the money is not the driving force in becoming a referee. It is the love of the game and the love of the kids playing the game. I still referee high school matches because I get exercise, I enjoy watching quality soccer (sometimes), and I feel like it is a service to my community. But, if I were being completely honest, I get the most pleasure out of refereeing the soccer matches for my grandchildren. No pay, just lots of smiles. Typically in a U-7 soccer match, I only say which team gets to throw it in, and, "Your shoe is untied." I learned very quickly that a six-year-old does NOT want help tying their shoes. They may take 3-4 minutes to accomplish this task, but true independence comes at a high price. I also learned my color scheme very quickly. One day I was the ref for Clara's team (my granddaughter), the Springer Spaniels. The ball went out of bounds and I signaled and said, "Pink's ball." Clara politely corrected me and said, "You made the same mistake with my sister. It is fuchsia, not pink, grampy!" You learn a lot as a referee, and as a grandparent.

Servant Leadership: Calling

Larry Spears (1995) writes that, individuals need to believe that you are willing to sacrifice self-interest for the good of the organization. Servant leaders have a natural desire to serve others. This notion of having a calling to serve is deeply rooted and values-based. The servant leaders desire to make a difference for others within the organization and will pursue opportunities to make a difference and to impact the lives of employees, the organization and the community — never for their own gain (Spears, 1995).

One of the most valuable lessons that youth must understand is sacrifice. They sacrifice their own glory, and number of goals, for the success of the team. Dishing off a pass to a team member in a better position to score is a sacrifice on an individual's part. The best soccer players pursue opportunities in the game to achieve shared goals, not for their own gain. Parents must understand this calling. When the parent is screaming for their child to score a goal, the better option for the team may be a pass. Parents who never stop talking don't allow the youth to make their own decisions, which deprives them of the valuable lesson called teamwork. Coming together is the beginning, staying together is the development and working together is the key to success.

My Son/Daughter is the Best Athlete Parent

Coaches tend to agree that the most challenging parents are the ones who played the game themselves. The worst of the worst are parents who played the game at the high school level but now can only dribble when they eat soup. These individuals are still scorned by the fact that no college, not even NAIA Division II, offered them a full ride. Parents that played at a college level typically are the best parents, because they have personally witnessed the worst behaviors from fans and do not want to emulate them. The high school soccer "pro" is trying to relive his/her past through their son or daughter. Be afraid, be very afraid.

You can probably spot the former athlete a mile away. They typically wear designer sweat pants (that barely fit), a t-shirt with the name of their high school team on it, and sun glasses, because they don't want to be ambushed by their adoring public, clamoring for autographs. They are always shouting from the touchline and acting as an un-official referee, waving imaginary yellow cards about and blowing their imaginary whistle, all while screaming directives to all the players. Their key focus is if their child were playing 100% of the time, there would not be any problems. Coach Chau said that one time a parent approached him before the start of the season, informing her that his son is a forward and needs to always play in that position. In fact, "if he is ever put in goal, we will leave the team." He then proceeded to give her a list of four other players that could play keeper/goalie if the starter ever got hurt or needed a replacement. We all know what happened next. Coach Chau put the young player in goal the very next game.

Coach Harry likes to call a certain type of adult, the "stop-watch parent." These are parents that believe their son or daughter is the best athlete and needs to play all the time, so they apparently keep a stop-watch to check on their kids' playing time. Coach Harry realized what was happening and had his manager keep track of minutes. It was no surprise, but the parent was consistently wrong. Then as the parent sent the coach the "exact" playing time of his son, the coach would return the email with the corrected time, explain the error, and not so subtlety indicate that this number was going to be decreasing if the "stop-watch" practice continued.

I was the AR (assistant referee) for a high school match a few years back. Homestead was playing Durango in a regular conference game. Nothing special, but the two teams were evenly matched, and it was a fun game to watch and participate in. The assistant coach for the Durango team obviously had a son on the team, which I cleverly deduced in a Sherlock Holmes sort of way: They had the same last name, same first name, and the coach kept calling him son, especially Jack Jr. This assistant coach was riding me the entire game because I was on his side of the field. At times, we were no more than a few feet apart. Nothing I called was appreciated, and calls that went against his team were wildly argued. I finally had enough and told the head coach that if he had another assistant coach, he "should warm him up because the one constantly talking to me is going to be gone very soon." I thought that this comment was clever, and certainly better than the alternative, which may have involved a felony on my part. Anyway, for the rest of the match the assistant was better, not great. Until the end of the match. The game went into overtime and there was a supposed "hand ball" in the box by Homestead. I did not think it was intentional and the center referee felt the same as me, so he motioned, "play on." You would think that the world had ended. Durango's assistant coach just lit me up. I think he even invented a few words in his verbal tirade, and the game ended with Homestead winning. Now as Paul Harvey would say, here is the rest of the story.

I am a college professor and teach graduate students in leadership. About one month after this soccer match, I had the pleasure of welcoming a new group of students into the University. You guessed it, the assistant coach from Durango was in my class. He did not immediately recognize me because I was out of uniform and in a completely different environment. Plus, I think he only saw the backside of my head on the pitch. But there was no mistaking him on my part. How can you forget the man responsible for yelling, "jumping Jehoshaphat," or some such phrase at me? I slowly took attendance in class and welcomed each student, until Mr. Jumping Jehoshaphat introduced himself. He was an assistant principal and assistant soccer coach. I inquired, "That's great, where do you coach?" He cocked his head, still trying to think where he knew me from, and he said, "Durango." My response again was, "Great, does your team ever play Homestead?" He said yes, and I could see the gears in his brain working overtime to figure this out. Soccer refs do not get opportunities like this very often, and I wanted to savor the moment. "So, how did your last match with Homestead go?" Almost there, the fish was on the line, and I just had to bring it into the boat "Not so well," he responded, "We lost in overtime." And now for the Piece de resistance, "Tell me, how was the officiating that game? Especially the AR on your side of the field?" Bingo. He turned white and sheepishly said, "He was great. Excellent in fact. My retort, "Hey, can I speak to you after class?" We did meet after class. He apologized, and I certainly extended the olive branch, indicating that soccer is soccer and the classroom is far removed from the green grass field at Homestead. Nevertheless, it did feel good at the end of the night.

Now, here is a piece of important research for all coaches and parents to read. Your daughter may be a great athlete, but let's get one thing straight, you cannot motivate her to do anything. In fact, research indicates that extrinsic motivation is counterproductive. Punishments and rewards are not really opposites, they serve the same function. Can external rewards, like paying a player every time she scores a goal, be productive? Yes, it temporarily teaches the player to work toward rewards, but once those rewards are gone, so is the motivation to play or even try. "At least two dozen studies have shown that people expecting to receive a reward for completing a task (or for doing it successfully) simply do not perform as well as those who expect nothing" (Kohn, 1994). Whether you believe it or not, research indicates that you cannot realistically motivate anybody for any extended period of time. So, stop trying parents. What you need to do is establish an environment that helps players intrinsically motivate themselves. In other words, by following the concepts of Servant Leadership, you can set up an atmosphere that promotes motivation and therefore assists with the learning process of the other skills associated with soccer. Thomas Edison is credited with saying that, "I have not failed. I've just found 10,000 ways that won't work."

Similar to Kohn, Deci and Ryan (2000), describe the use of rewards as "control through seduction." Control is defined as the use of pressure or enticements to achieve an end result. Basically, anything that parents do TO soccer players rather than working WITH them is control. The bottom line is that research indicates that yelling at a soccer player is detrimental, while working with the young players practicing skills is the key to success, so they intrinsically learn to love the game. In other words, no amount of screaming, yelling, blaming, etc. will create any significant change for your kids. So, stop doing this, and you might possibly want to "get a life!"

I had not heard the phrase, "Professionalization of Youth Sports," until doing research on this book. But in a short time, it became painfully obvious what it was. (This is the part where I sound really old—mainly because I am.) When I was a child, we all played three or four sports. We had volunteer coaches (my dad) and played for the fun of the sport. We had football season, basketball season, golf season, and so on. Today, kids are expected to play one sport all year long. Also, if you do not start playing soccer at age five, good luck making the high school team—it is not going to happen. Parents pay hundreds of dollars an hour for "professional" coaches. Kids are getting private lessons in their sport of choice, along with speed drills, special camps, and so on. Once you reach a certain age and skill level, you are expected to join a travelling team. In this case, travelling does not mean jump in a car and drive one hour to the tournament, it means jump on a plane (pay for it), get a hotel for the weekend, figure out what you are going to do about your "other" kids that have to stay home, and spend thousands of dollars sitting in the rain and 40 degree weather to watch six soccer matches in two days. Professionalism refers to getting paid to play a sport, and parents are under the false impression that success in sports is a natural gateway to getting into the best college, and then into the best graduate school, so they can get the best job. Parents believe the stakes are extremely high, so it is no wonder they put such pressure on their kids early in life. Given the "professional" nature of youth soccer, one parent tweeted: "Playing team sports is a great way for kids to experience getting yelled at outside of the home."

Servant Leadership:
Nurturing the Spirit - JOY!!

Larry Spears writes that, "the servant leader is some-one who understands the deep human need to contribute to personally meaningful enterprises. The servant-leader nurtures the individual's spirit through honest praise and supportive recognition. Criticisms and suggestions are not personal or harsh. The joy of the work is celebrated through means that acknowledge the value of employees' commitment to worthwhile activities. The servant leader reminds employees to reflect on the importance of both the struggles and successes in the organization and learn from both" (Rockwood Preparatory Academy, n.d. para. 12).

Parents have a natural instinct to take care of their children, which obviously means to protect them. However, one of the challenges of being a parent is knowing when to protect and when to let them go. You know that you are a helicopter parent when you have your son's soccer coach on speed dial and you keep a list of things to tell him the next time you call.

A 2014 study by Yale professor William Deresiewicz found that children with helicopter parents have less executive function capabilities. He found that these children have a hard time changing activities, delaying gratification, and controlling their emotions. These capabilities predict future wealth, health, and academic success. Consequently, students with helicopter parents have a higher tendency to struggle in college... and in life (Deresiewicz, 2015).

Peter M. Jonas, Ph.D.

The Abusive Parent

Tony, a coach for FC, said that the worst incident of abuse was on his U-14 club team. He had a player who was very talented and a father who was, let's just say, "very excitable." The father was about 6'6" and had previously played soccer in Europe. During one match, the score was tied at 0-0, and FC was playing against a big rival. The father, of course, thought that the sun rose and set on his son's ability. He also, of course, thought that Tony didn't utilize his son's ability to the best advantage. His son got tangled up with another player; they were kicking at each other. The ref called a foul on the opposing player, and while the ref was sorting out the foul, the father decided to walk out onto the field and take things into his own hands. At 6'6", he stood over the kid of the opposing team, who was about 14 years of age, and proceeded to yell at him in another language. When the ref came to stop the abuse, he hurled the same abuse at the referee. The referee was taken aback, but said if the father didn't leave the field, the game was going to be ended... or actually, if he didn't leave the entire park, the game would be called off. Coach Tony tried to intervene. He told the father to leave and that if he didn't, FC was going to lose the game. Unfortunately, the father kept saying, "I no care! I no care!" Eventually a couple of the other fathers on the team escorted him off the field. His parting shot for the entire soccer club was to give the finger as he walked off into the distance. The sad part, of course, was his child crying after the game. How do you console a child when, no matter what, he must go back to that father? All Coach Tony told the player was that, "Your dad shouldn't have done what he did, but he's your father and he means well and cares about you." Unfortunately, the player left the team, and who knows if the father learned any lesson from the incident. This is a reminder that: 1) it is only a game and world peace does not revolve around a U-14 match, and 2) the game is about the kids, not the parents.

Harry is also a coach for FC, and he related a story where a parent called his house after a game. It was an important game, and her daughter had not played. FC is a select soccer club, and in an important match, everybody knows it's a possibility that every player might not get in the game. In this particular game, the young lady did not play. Coach Harry got a call at his house from this irate parent, but Harry's future mother-in-law answered. The parent promptly told the mother-in-law what an awful person Harry was and that he wasn't an honest person. This was a case of not only the person bashing the coach, but taking out her frustration on an innocent person—Who, by the way, knew nothing about soccer. After about 10 minutes of this parent yelling obscenities, coach Harry came home, and his mother-in-law handed the phone over to Harry and calmly said, "I think this is for you."

Then there is the story of an East Rockaway soccer mom angered over being dropped from the team's e-mail list. Because the mother did not receive directions for the soccer match, she took it out on the coach. According to the police report, the mother was arrested after slamming a metal folding chair across the face of her daughter's coach. There are a number of sordid details to this story, but the two key ones are that a woman, a fully grown adult, hit a soccer coach with a chair because she was dropped from the email list. Let that sink in. The woman allegedly committed this action in front of her 12-year-old daughter, and the cherry on top of the story is that the coach was a volunteer "who stepped up to coach the team when no one else would."

In another incident involving a mother, Nick Kyonka, a staff reporter for the *Star* (2007), wrote an article entitled, "Irate Soccer Mom Brings Game to Screeching Halt":

> It's Sunday afternoon and a semifinal soccer match is dissolving into screaming and shoving. A referee is accosted, a supporter punched, a police officer – who tries to intervene – scratched. Arrests are made, and an embarrassed team is withdrawn from the tournament.

> Think we're talking about World Cup play? Not even close. These histrionics took place at an "under-8" match for boys in Pickering on the weekend. The referee? A 14-year-old girl.

> Now, an irate soccer mom who disagreed with the girl's officiating faces assault charges. Her husband is also charged.

> "Incidents like this are very rare and sometime parents get heated or passionate about the game," said Shelly Augustin of the Pickering Soccer Club. "It's an incident and it's unfortunate that it happened but we had people on hand who were able to handle it quickly."

The outburst came during the dying moments of a semifinal match of the kids' tournament, in Diana, Princess of Wales Park near Kingston Rd. and Brock Rd., police said.

A team from Hillcrest had battled a team from Wexford, and were moments away from winning the game when the mother of a Hillcrest player took exception to a call by the teenaged ref.

When the referee's father tried to intervene to protect her, the woman allegedly punched him in the face, yelling at both of them.

That's when off-duty Durham Region police Det. Tom Dingwall, who was watching a game on an opposite field, overheard the commotion and decided to investigate.

"I was there watching a game and identified myself and arrested the female for assault," said Dingwall. "She began resisting, pulling away and digging her nails into my hand and her husband became involved and began pulling me away from his wife."

Both the woman and man were arrested, but worse was the message sent to the kids, Dingwall said.

Imagine watching a soccer match that is tied after regulation and goes into penalty kicks to determine winner. Very exciting, right? Now imagine that a father walks directly behind the goal to stand there during the penalty kicks. Of course, the referee politely asks the gentleman to leave and surprisingly, he does not. In fact, he yells to the young ref: "I can stand wherever the [expletive] I want to. You can't tell me what to do." The ref stops the game and refuses to continue until the adult—and I use this term loosely—leaves the field. Parents from both sides join in telling the man to leave, and he not only refuses, but hits the ref and a brawl ensues between the spectator and the people trying to defend the ref (Mattison, 2000).

Police are called, the game is cancelled and pretty much everyone leaves frustrated, especially the instigator who is led away in cuffs for assault. All for a U-7 game. This is not a misprint, a U-7 game. Now this was a tournament, so obviously there were high stakes involved—including a four-inch trophy made out of plastic. Of course, banning parents from youth sports is one option. In Georgia, the South Cherokee County Recreation Association banned nine parents for life from the complex because of fighting and name calling. This was at a U-10 soccer match. Unfortunately, these stories are way too commonplace in today's youth soccer, or pretty much any youth sport. I just wish adults had this much energy when it came to voting or volunteering at their local schools.

There is even a website dedicated to protecting officials and helping them file lawsuits against parents. The world has now officially gone off its axis. Http://Ur-safe. org is a site "developed to educate athletes, administrators of sports programs, fans, and the public on the importance of sportsmanship on the fields of play and advocate for all sports officials young and old. It is our wish for this site to be utilized as a resource in leading legislative efforts in the protection of sports officials around the world" (https://ur-safe.org/). If at first you don't succeed, sue them.

The Abusive Parent usually has a plethora of jabs he/she can bring, and bring them they do. "Come on are you blind?" Knowing full well that the referee can, in fact, see… but apparently this 13-year-old girl ref has an unknown bias toward the coach of the Wildcats and needs the other U-7 team to win for no apparent or logical reason. The insulter is not usually embarrassed, nor will they typically relent for any reason. For the Insulter-Parent, an "idiot" ref is always an idiot, and the coach that is "clueless" will remain clueless throughout eternity. Once the insulter starts, there is no turning back, much like the ride into the Valley of Death.

After a regional tournament, Coach Chris was walking back to his car and overheard a parent talking to his son from the same soccer club but a different age group. The parent proceeded to drop the F-bomb about 34 times in describing his, "big f--ing important regional team. Big regional team player can't even f--ing play a good game. Can't f—ing play for more than twenty minutes without getting tired. Big f—ing star. You should be f—ing embarrassed with yourself." What parent does this to a 16-year-old boy? By the way, the young man took it all in stride, and then after about 10 minutes simply turned to his father and said, "Thanks for the positive motivation. Can we go get something to f—ing eat now?"

What's in a name? A family from the Ohio Valley had a very talented son, Pat. Of course, the parents wanted the best coaching for their rising star, but when Pat was assigned to Coach Steve, the parents needed to talk with the Club's president. The parents politely explained to the president that Coach Steve is a great person but not a good "fit" for Pat. "You see, Pat has special skills and special goals that can only be addressed by Coach Ronaldo." (This was not really his name, if you have not surmised that by now.) The Club president knew exactly what the parents wanted. While Pat was American, and coach Steve was American, coach Ronaldo was "foreign." We all know that foreign coaches are better than American coaches. Names mean everything. (Just in case this was not obvious, the last two sentences are filled with sarcasm). There are a number of research studies that demonstrate how a person's name can create bias in individuals. I am not going to get into that research here, but suffice it to say that a friend and colleague, Marijuana Smith (not her last name, but her first name really is Marijuana), has people immediately forming judgements before they know her. By the way, she has a doctorate in education and never stops smiling. Back to the story. The parents of Pat simply believed that someone with the name Ronaldo was a much better coach than Steve, based on no facts other than a name. Pat stayed with coach Steve and the team made it to regionals that year. Pat made great strides as a player and team mate. Coaches need to coach, players need to play, and parents need to stay the hell out of the way.

El Paso, Texas has a population of approximately 700,000 people. In 1999, the city witnessed a series of incidents that included parents from one team pulling knives, attacking parents of players on opposing teams, and verbally and physically abusing young players. Enough was enough so, "Paula Powell, sports operations supervisor for the city, and Keith Wilson, a psychotherapist with experience as a soccer administrator, coach and referee, developed the Sports Parent Training Program." The program soon became mandatory before any child could participate in a city-sponsored sport. At least one parent of a youth athlete must attend the program. In the three-hour program, parents learn "performance skills to help them cope with the intensity of their feelings. They learn communication skills and sports rules. It sounds like spectator boot camp." And it works, the number of parent incidents, and simply the decibel level on the sidelines of soccer matches as well as other sports, declined precipitously. For example, the city's "zero-tolerance" policy of abuse was tested when a father charged the field to shout at an official. He was banned for a year (Manalapan Soccer Club, 2014).

The Eastbay Soccer Association had one 13-year-old referee relate the following story. He was the ref for a U-8 summer soccer league. First, most U-8 players are not always familiar with the rules, and I would have to say that 95.3% of their parents are not either. Anyway, one parent decided that he had enough and started yelling at the young ref, informing him what he was doing "wrong." Very calmly and with a certain amount of confidence, this 13-year-old explained that, "I had to talk to some parents and tell them to calm down a little bit." What actually happened was a 13-year-old boy stopped a U-8 soccer match and coolly walked over to a 48-year-old adult twice his size to lecture him on maturity and priorities in life. The young man then peacefully returned to the game. It must be noted that this ref was making about $10 an hour for being a referee. This type of action sort of puts a smile on your face, doesn't it?

Servant Leadership

Bruce Brownlee, an experienced referee from Atlanta had the best advice I have ever read. He wrote that parents should only say six things to their young soccer players.

Before the Match

1. I love you.
2. Good luck.
3. Have fun.

After the Match

1. I love you.
2. It was great to see you play.
3. What would you like to eat?

Lessons Learned

Facts about Sports

Here are a few facts that detail the positive aspects for kids playing sports. A plethora of studies indicate that high school students that play sports:

1. are far less likely to drop out of school.
2. consistently receive higher grades.
3. have improved concentration and classroom behavior.
4. are 15 percent more likely to attend college.
5. (for women) are 73 percent more likely to earn a college degree within six years of graduating high school.
6. demonstrate more confidence, leadership, and self-respect.
7. have a better appreciation for diversity and a more developed sense of morality.
8. tend to earn significantly higher incomes than those who did not.

9. were less likely to use drugs, smoke cigarettes and carry a weapon (At Your Own Risk, 2018).

Lessons from a Referee

Let's end this book on another positive note. As a youth soccer referee, these are the 10 lessons I learned over the years.

1. First, I learned to be patient. I learned to be patient when coaches or parents were yelling at me. I learned patience waiting for players to move back 10 yards for substitutions and leaving the field if their team was winning, and patience with parents at every level and every day.

2. I learned that when the ball goes out of bounds in a girls' soccer match, only a player from the team that deserves the throw-in goes after the ball. But, in a boys' soccer match, one player from each of the two teams goes after the ball in hopes they can convince or fool me that it is their throw-in.

3. I learned that the best laid plans of mice and men are thrown out the window. I would plan for a clear, warm day and it would rain, and a cold front would always come through. I would plan for a quiet game between two schools and all hell breaks loose.

4. I learned no parent knows the off-side rule and no parent can accurately tell time.

5. As a youth soccer ref, I learned how to tie shoes, and more importantly, I learned how to watch a four-year-old tie her shoe.

6. I learned that many younger players are more interested in flowers, birds, singing, and skipping than kicking a ball.

7. I also grew eyes out of the back of my head because you need this in any match.

8. I learned how to command, bribe, threaten, plead, and negotiate with parents.

9. I learned that soccer is exercise and soccer is fun. Anytime you can have an activity that combines these two, the benefits are unlimited.

10. Finally, I learned that soccer is really fun without parents.

Lessons from Coaches

Here is a list of things that youth soccer coaches say they learned from soccer:

1. Don't act like the parents of your players

2. Sportsmanship is not part of the game, it IS the game

3. Ability to deal with failure

4. Discipline is important on and off the field

5. How to practice and the value of practice

6. Teamwork is important on and off the field

7. Relationships: importance of developing relationships

8. Value of rules/guidelines

9. How to win and how to lose. The two are not that different when it comes to lessons learned.

10. How to deal with success

11. How to take feedback—coaches can be brutally honest with players and parents—and this is a good thing

12. A great coach seldom talks about soccer

Lessons from Youth Soccer Players

Now here is a list of things that kids say they want the parents to do, especially the parents that coach their team (gleaned from comments by Sports Illustrated for Kids readers).

1. Know the game. So, you think your son or daughter will be delighted to have you for a coach just because it means you can spend some "quality time" together? Wrong! If you don't know what you're talking about on the field—and you don't make the effort to learn—they would rather you just stay home.

2. Listen to your players. Kids like to feel respected. Yes, you need to establish your authority—to keep both kids and parents in line—but players are people too. "My mom listens to us and our ideas. That's why she's a great coach," wrote one kid.

3. Don't play favorites. For most kids, being the coach's pet is bad enough; being one just because of bloodlines is unbearable. On the other hand, no child wants to be singled out for extra harsh treatment because Dad's the coach. As hard as it may be at times, treat your child like any other player. "Nobody is more important than anyone else," wrote a child in an SI for Kids readers' poll.

4. Get everyone in the game. All kids like to win. But more than winning, kids like to play. Make sure all

your players get plenty of playing time and opportunities to try different positions.

5. Make it fun, Part I. The No. 1 reason kids play sports is to have fun. You can help. Turn repetitive drills into good-humored contests. Make games exciting, not terrifying. Treat the team to pizza or ice cream after a game now and then.

6. Make it fun, Part II. Enjoy yourself. Kids don't want to feel like a burden. "My dad's a great coach because he always has a good time," one child reported.

7. Don't baby them. No kid wants to do 100 sit-ups or run 50 laps, but players expect the coach to make them do whatever they need to do to be ready for the game.

8. Be a teacher. Kids play sports for fun, but if they don't improve, they'll eventually get bored or frustrated, and perhaps quit. Help them learn skills, rules, and strategy so that they can maximize their abilities.

9. Act your age. It's embarrassing for kids when their parents argue with officials and yell obscenities. It's even worse when the parent is the coach. Keep your anger in check and your language decent.

10. Care—but not too much. Kids want their activities to be taken seriously, but not too seriously. "She did not care if I won or lost," and, "He's not too emotional," were the most common reasons kids gave for why their mom or dad was a great coach (TOP 10 Tips for Coaching Your Child's Team, no date).

One Final Story

Ethan Zohn thinks that "Soccer is the most democratic sport in the world. It's accessible to everyone."

Ethan Zohn is a Vassar College graduate who played professional soccer in Zimbabwe and the United States, coached college soccer at Fairleigh Dickinson University, and in 2003, was Head Coach of the U.S. National Maccabiah team at the Pan-American Maccabiah Games in Santiago, Chile. In addition, he was the 2002 winner of "Survivor," the reality TV show that has the philosophy of seeing who can outwit, outplay, and outlast everyone else.

With his prize money, Ethan co-founded Grassroots Soccer, a nonprofit organization that trains professional soccer players to teach children in Africa about HIV/AIDS prevention. Zohn is quoted as saying:

> Soccer teaches young people the value of hard work, being a team player, communicating clearly, and being smart on the field and in life. On the soccer field, you get out what you put in. That's true off the field too. Maybe most importantly, soccer teaches self-confidence, something that is incredibly important for young people, particularly those that are marginalized by society due to their economic status, gender, HIV status, and more. Soccer gives young people the tools they need to become leaders. This is exactly what we do at Grassroots Soccer and it makes me hopeful every day (U.S. Soccer Federation, 2014).

Servant Leadership

Robert Greenleaf, the founder of Servant Leadership, explained that servant leaders want to serve first, and then conscious choice brings one to aspire to lead. Servant leaders: 1) care for others; 2) have an ability to set an example; 3) have a commitment to uphold ethics; and 4) drive to support others to success. If parents would follow these four simple concepts, they would not only help their young athletes in soccer, but also in life.

Youth soccer coaches know that the sport is important, but the 12 different aspects of servant leadership are more important as the young players grow from being dependent youth to independent leaders:

1. Listening
2. Empathy
3. Healing
4. Awareness
5. Persuasion
6. Conceptualization
7. Foresight
8. Stewardship
9. Growth
10. Building Community
11. Calling
12. Nurturing the Spirit - JOY!!

The bottom line is coaches need to be allowed to coach. Parents need to be quiet. And kids need to have fun and know you love them. It is quite simple.

What is soccer? It has been described as a game with 22 players, two linesmen and 500 referees—depending on the number of parents at a game.

Figure 1: Neuroscience and Soccer: Brain of Soccer Mom

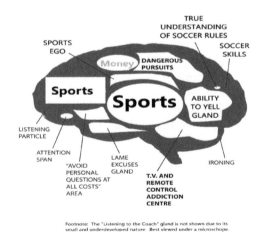

Figure 2: Neuroscience and Soccer: Brain of Soccer Dad

Conclusions

UNDERSTAND THE STATE OF THE GAME

It is estimated that youth sports are a $17 billion business, which is larger than the NFL. Unfortunately, participation is declining from 41 percent in 2011 to 37 percent in 2017. Moreover, approximately 75 percent of children who play organized sports quit by age 13. No one is really sure why youth sports are on the decline, whether it is lack of interest, kids playing video games, or fear of injury, e.g., concern over CTE.

However, the story is not the same for all families. A report in *The Atlantic* in 2018, stated that participation in sports for wealthy families is actually on the rise. For example, for families that earn less than $25,000, the number of children playing sports has decreased from 42 to 34 percent, while in families earning more than $100,000, the number has increased from 2011 to 2017 by 3 percent (66% to 69%). What has happened is the rise of elite or travel teams. In soccer this can start as early as 11 years old. The team is not only traveling out of state but to multiple states to play in "Best of the Best" tournaments. Just joining these teams can cost thousands of dollars each year, and the disparity has created super teams that win all the trophies, leaving behind many players who simply lose interest in the game (Thompson, 2018). Money is a difference maker.

You cannot blame a parent for wanting to help their child. The system has many flaws as well. In the 1990s, colleges spent approximately $250 million a year in athletic scholarships, but this figure has risen to over $3 billion because of increased media, television, etc. It does not stop there because some colleges have athletes who are "one and done." They attend school for one year before turning pro. Students that use athletics to make a better life for themselves see the system as working just fine, but this is by far the minority of athletes. Parents need to know the facts when it comes to playing sports.

Know the Rules of the Game

There are only 17 laws for soccer. These are not rules, or guidelines, they are laws. You really have to love the terminology. Some organizations have made local modifications to the laws, and there are adjustments for the age of the participants, but generally these 17 laws are what parents need to learn.

"The rules of soccer are very simple, basically it is this: if it moves, kick it. If it doesn't move, kick it until it does." —Phil Woosnam

Listed below is the official language of the International Football Association Board (IFAB) followed by a more generic interpretation.

Law 1: The Field of Play

IFAB rule: Soccer can be played on either grass or artificial turf, but the surface must be green in color. The field must be rectangular in shape, and distinctly marked by two short goal lines and two long-touch lines. The field is divided into halves, separated by the halfway line, which runs from the midpoints of each touchline. At the midpoint of the halfway line is a marked center point surrounded by a lined center circle with a radius of 10 yards. Opposing players are not allowed to enter this circle during the possessing team's kick-off. The length of the touch line must be greater than the length of the goal line. There also must be a five foot high flag in each corner, although this is one of the rules that gets glossed over many times.

What Parents Really Need to Know

Parents need to sit on one side of the field and the players sit on the other side of the field, AWAY from the parents. I am pretty sure you know why. However, many parents take this positioning as a challenge to yell even louder so little Bobby can hear them.

Today, many soccer fields are surfaced with artificial turf. There are many reasons for this, but the principle explanation is that someone wants as many tiny little rubber plugs to get into my shoes as possible. Soccer is a much faster game on artificial turf, and it has been found to be better for injuries, but it is obviously far more expensive than grass and does take its toll, wearing out shoes and equipment faster. Artificial turfs do afford a rich alumnus the opportunity to have a field named after them.

Law 2: The Ball

IFAB rule: A soccer ball must be spherical in shape and made of leather or another comparable medium. Its circumference must be in the range of 27 to 28 inches. This rule is only applicable for official sanctioned matches, as youth leagues often employ the use of a smaller ball that is better suited to children.

What Parents Really Need to Know

Typically, parents do not complain about the soccer balls, although I have seen my fair share of parents and coaches take out their frustrations on an innocent ball by kicking or punching it. Parents should know all about soccer balls because they have to buy a new one every week, or so it seems. Youth play with different size balls because they are easier to control (the balls, not the kids) and to learn the game with. What you may not know is that stealing balls is not just a practice for the soccer match. Practice is one big smorgasbord of soccer ball sharing, paring, and thieving. Some of this is actually unintentional, but kids know if they go to practice with one ball, they need to come home with one ball. It does not matter if it is a different color, brand, or style, the number is the only thing that counts for parents. This is why you will see every smart soccer player writing their name on the ball in glow-in-the-dark, deep and very, very large font.

Law 3: The Number of Players

IFAB rule: Matches are generally played by two teams of 11 to a side. The goalkeeper is included in the 11-player total. If a team cannot field at least seven players at match time, the game is a forfeit. Teams of fewer than 11 a side can often be seen in youth leagues where smaller teams are used as a developmental tool. FIFA-sanctioned matches are generally limited to three substitutions per match, with the exception of friendly matches. Most youth leagues allow an unlimited number of substitutions, which must also be listed on the game card prior to the beginning of the match, otherwise those players are ineligible. Substitutions may only enter at the halfway line, upon the referee's approval, and after the player being subbed out has left the pitch. The goalkeeper may be substituted with anyone on the pitch or any eligible substitute on the bench during a game stoppage.

What Parents Really Need to Know

Same as the size of the ball, the number of players does depend on the age of participants. The younger the player, the smaller the ball, the smaller the field, and the lower number of people on the pitch at any one time. The reason for this is to maximize the number of touches each person gets and hopefully to teach players how to control the ball as opposed to simply just kicking it in any direction. (For more information, see the explanation of "Big kick" in a previous section).

The best way to remember the number of players is 7-11, like the convenience store. A team has to have at least seven players to start the match, but 11 is the maximum.

Law 4: The Players' Equipment

IFAB rule: All players are required to wear a jersey, shorts, shin guards, socks, and cleats. The socks must cover the shin guards entirely. If the referee deems a player's equipment unsatisfactory, the player can be sent off until the issue is remedied. Coaches can also receive a yellow card for players not properly equipped.

What Parents Really Need to Know

There is no jewelry allowed when playing soccer, including earrings, nose rings, belly rings, bracelets, or tiaras. Medical bracelets are the only exception to the rule. A rubber bracelet that your boyfriend gave you has to come off. These are all safety issues. Moreover, referees do not care that you just got your ear pierced one day ago and were told to keep the starter stud in your ear or it will close up. It must come out. Covering it with tape does no good. Is the hole really going to close in one hour? I don't think so.

No shoes, no shirt, no soccer. A player must have the proper gear, including shin guards, which surprisingly is one of the more controversial pieces of equipment. For some reason soccer players, especially the older ones, try to get away with wearing really small shin guards, certainly not FIFA approved. I am not sure if this is a fashion statement or if the shin guards are restrictive, but I can't count the number of times a shin guard fell onto the field during play and it looked more like a credit card than the required guard.

Footwear

Don't get me started on footwear. In the United States we call soccer shoes cleats, but elsewhere in the world they are boots. To Americans the idea of a boot is something you wear in Wisconsin during the winter. In the United Kingdom a cleat is also known as a stud, but in the U.S. a stud is someone like Jason Momoa. By the way parents, there is no FIFA rule about having to wear the most expensive or color coordinated boot in the world. That $300 pair of cleats really can be a pair of $20 tennis shoes.

Dangerous Equipment and Dad

The key to soccer equipment is that it needs to protect the player and not be dangerous to others, i.e., no earrings or sharp spikes. Parents, here is what NOT to do. The *New York Times* reported that Dr. Stephen Cito (yes, a doctor) allegedly sharpened the chin strap of his son's football helmet in an obvious effort to gain an advantage on the competition. Five kids from the opposing team were slashed, with one needing 12 stitches. The officials stopped the game because of the injuries. The son was expelled from school and the father received probation, 400 hours of community service, and a few days in jail. After his punishment, he was free to go back to his profession, which was serving as a dentist for children. Maybe he was just trying to drum up some new business?

Law 5: The Referee

IFAB rule: The referee is the authority on the field, and his word is law. If you question a referee's decision, you can be disciplined further simply for dissent.

What Parents Really Need to Know

Please read the first sentence of Law #5, the referee is the authority on the field, and his word is law—enough said.

Reasons for Becoming a Soccer Referee

You love football but can't quite understand the rules.

You have the strange desire to run aimlessly around in the wind, rain, hail and snow.

You love the sound of verbal abuse.

You find it hard to make decisions, and whenever you do, you're always wrong.

You enjoy changing your clothes in out houses.

Refs Are Dedicated

Despite the information listed above, the majority of soccer referees are well-versed in the rules and dedicated to the sport. They certainly are not doing it for the money, which typically is something like $10 to $40 per game even on the high school level. Take, for example, the following story about a dedicated ref.

One day right in the middle of a match, Robert Gayle, a noted soccer referee, suddenly blew his whistle to stop play. Robert stopped to bow his head as a long funeral procession passed by on the road that ran alongside the field.

"Wow," said one of the parents on the sideline. "That is the most thoughtful and touching thing I've ever seen. You truly are a kind man. I'll never think badly of a referee again."

Robert replied, "Thanks, we were married nearly 30 years."

The final point is that, believe it or not, referees are humans too. They feel some emotion after being yelled at. One time I calculated that I make about $10 per hour, or .10 cents per insult, for any match.

Law 6: The Assistant Referees

IFAB rule: The assistant referees are primarily responsible for assisting the referee in performing his or her duties—this includes signaling with a flag when a ball goes out of play, when a player is fouled, or when a player is offside.

What Parents Really Need to Know

Assistant referees may actually have it harder than the center ref. They are closer to the coaches or the parents. Sometimes, they are right next to the parents on the sideline, which apparently is the same as holding up a sign that says, "Please yell at me, because I am close to you and enjoy it so much."

In case you did not know, the assistant referee is also called the linesman and has very specific duties. They do not just indicate if the ball went out of bounds or not, they also are the main person responsible for off side and calling any infractions in their section of the field to assist the center ref. They also get to hold flags, which is simply cool and powerful. Recently FIFA introduced us to the VAR or

Video Assistant Referee. This is really instant replay for soccer, but I appreciate calling a computer an assistant referee, it makes it more human. However, it does take the fun out of yelling at a camera and not a person.

Law 7: The Duration of the Match

IFAB rule: A soccer match is comprised of two 45-minute halves, with extra time added at the referee's discretion. The halves are separated by a half-time period not to exceed 15 minutes. The extra time generally corresponds with the referee's determination of how much time was taken up due to substitutions and injuries. Although soccer does have an allotted time limit, it is ultimately up to the referees when to end a match.

What Parents Really Need to Know

When you are winning the match, time goes slower than normal and when you are losing, the time seems to fly by. Nevertheless, the key to the IFAB rule is that time can be added per the discretion of the referee. I hate to break it to parents, but if your son has the ball and his team is losing by one goal and he is attacking, "ready" to score, the ref can blow the whistle to end the match. Refs do not have to wait for a break in the action or allow any play to continue if time is up. Referees are also supposed to stop the clock on injuries and after scores, but I will let you in on a secret, too many referees let the clock run way too often after goals because they want the game to end faster. This is not the correct way to operate, but it happens.

Law 8: The Start and Restart of Play

IFAB rule: Kick-off is generally determined by a coin toss, whereby the winning team can either choose to start with the ball or choose which goal they would like to attack. The losing team is then afforded whatever choice the winner does not elect to take. Kick-off occurs at the start of each half, and after each goal scored, and is taken at the center of the halfway line. If a team scores a goal, the opposing team is given the kick-off to restart the match.

What Parents Really Need to Know

For any kickoff, the ball is placed in the center of the field and all players must be on their own half of the field. Players from the receiving team need to be at least 10 yards from the ball, or in other words, outside of the center circle on the field. Previously, the ball had to move forward, but this rule recently changed and it can now be kicked backwards, which obviously helps the offensive team. The person kicking the ball cannot touch it twice in a row. I wish I had a nickel for every time I had to explain the kick off rules for a U-9 team or younger.

Law 9: The Ball In and Out of Play

IFAB rule: The ball is out of play when it fully crosses either the goal line or the touch line. It is also out of play if the referee stops play for any reason. If, for any reason, the ball strikes the frame of the goal or the referee and remains within the goal and touch lines, it is still in play.

What Parents Really Need to Know

There are two things for parents to know about this law. The first is that the entire ball has to go over the line to be considered out—the ENTIRE ball. More importantly, if I am the assistant referee, I am probably 5 to 10 feet away from the ball, and as a parent in the stands, you are 50 to 100 yards away. So, why do you think you have a better view of if the ball went out or not or who touched it?

Law 10: The Method of Scoring

IFAB rule: A goal is scored when the entire ball has crossed the goal line within the frame of the goal. At the end of the match, the team with the most goals is the winner, barring the circumstantial necessity for extra time.

What Parents Really Need to Know

See my notes from Law #9. Again, I am closer to the action and can decide if the entire ball went in the net or not. If your son or daughter scores a goal, world peace will not transpire and poverty will not be vanish, so there is no need to jump up and down screaming. I can understand the excitement if the score is 1-0, but when it becomes 4-0 or 10-0, the screaming and cheering are over the top. From speaking comes repentance and from listening comes wisdom. Although Bill Shankly, the Liverpool manager, said, "Some people believe football is a matter of life and death. I'm very disappointed with that attitude. I can assure you it is much, much more important than that."

One of the best soccer stories in history is when Chris Nicholl, a defender for Aston Villa, scored four goals in one game on March 20, 1976. The only problem is that he scored two goals for Aston Villa and two "own goals," so the game ended in 2-2 draw. To make matters even worse, the referee would not give him the game ball because it was his last match and he wanted the ball.

Law 11: Offside

IFAB rule: When an attacking player receives the ball while on his opponent's half, he must be level or behind the second to last defender (the last typically being the goalkeeper). However, this rule only applies if he is involved with the play.

What Parents Really Need to Know

Alright, this is where it gets interesting. Typically, off-side is only called for U-8 or older teams, so parents should start learning the rule now, it will take 30 or 35 years to get it right. By my estimations, 75% of all players know the rule, 63% of coaches, and 1% of all parents.

An offensive, or attacking player, can't be ahead of the ball and involved in the play unless there is a defender between him and the goalkeeper. Basically, you cannot be "basket hanging" or waiting by the goal for someone to pass you the ball. Players cannot be offside on a corner kick, goal kick or throw in. (I am not sure why, but this is the Law from the soccer gods.) A player can be in the off-side position but not offside. Notice the word "position" in the previous sentence. FIFA indicates that a player is in an offside position if he is nearer to his opponents' goal line than both the ball and the second to last opponent.

For example, team A has the ball and is attacking the goal of team B. A2 is a player from team A and in an off-side position. A1 has the ball, shoots, and scores with A2 in the offside position but not involved in the play. Goal or no goal? The answer is goooooooooaaaaaallllllllll. If A2 is not involved in the play, that makes it a legal play and the goal counts. Here is the question, what does it mean that he is not involved in the play? The answer is, "it is up to the discretion of the referee." But if A2 is just standing still, he is not involved in the play. If A2 is charging the goal, he is probably involved in the play.

Consider the same scenario where team A has the ball and is attacking the goal of team B. A2 is a player from team A and in an offside position but not involved with the play. A1 has the ball and shoots, but this time the ball bounces off the cross bar and A2 gets the rebound and kicks it in the goal. Goal or no goal? The answer is no goal.

A2 is obviously now involved in the play, and when it was originally kicked, he was in the offside position. Even if A2 is now onside, this is still an illegal play.

OK, clear as mud now? Let's examine the exceptions to the rule; "I before e: except after "c." A player cannot be offside if he is on his half of the field when the ball is kicked. Here is the part that most parents do not understand: to be considered offside it is when the ball is kicked, not when the player receives the ball. If a player is in the offside position when the ball is kicked but runs backwards to receive it in the onside position, she is still offside. The most important thing to remember is that this is the main job of two assistant referees who are 10 to 20 times closer to the field than you are. Again, I am pretty sure the ARs (assistant referees) have a much better view than the parents. It is sort of like when you are watching a football game and know the professional coach of 20 years is making a mistake because you know what to do from your years of watching football on TV.

Here is the best explanation for offside. You're in a shoe shop, second in line for the checkout. Behind the shop assistant, near the register, is a pair of shoes which you have seen and which you must have. The female shopper in front of you has seen them also and is eyeing them with desire. Both of you have forgotten your purses. It would be totally rude to push in front of the first woman if you had no money to pay for the shoes. The shop assistant remains at the cash register, waiting. Your friend is trying on another pair of shoes at the back of the shop and sees your dilemma and decides to throw her purse to you. If she does, you can catch the purse, then walk round the other shopper and buy the shoes. If you are really coordinated, she could throw the purse ahead of the other shopper and, while it is in flight, you could jump around the other shopper, catch the purse and buy the shoes. But, always remember that until the purse has actually been thrown, it would be plain wrong to be forward of the other shopper (Madden, no date). This is the offside rule for women. Sorry, it is fairly sexist of an explanation, but it is funny.

Law 12: Fouls and Misconduct

- IFAB rule: A direct free kick is awarded when a player:
- Kicks or attempts to kick an opponent
- Trips or attempts to trip an opponent
- Jumps at an opponent
- Charges an opponent
- Strikes or attempts to strike an opponent
- Pushes an opponent
- Tackles an opponent
- Holds an opponent
- Spits at an opponent
- Handles the ball deliberately

If any of these fouls are committed by a player in their team's penalty area, the opposing team is awarded a penalty kick. Indirect free kicks are awarded if a player:

- Plays in a dangerous manner
- Impedes the progress of an opponent
- Prevents the goalkeeper from releasing the ball from his/her hands
- Commits any other unmentioned offense

Bob Paisly once said, "If you're in the penalty area and don't know what to do with the ball, put it in the net and we'll discuss the options later."

Yellow cards are awarded as a caution or warning to a player and can be issued for the following offenses:

- Unsporting behavior
- Dissent by word or action
- Persistent infringement of the Laws of the Game
- Delaying the restart of play
- Failure to respect the required distance when play is restarted with a corner kick, free kick, or throw-in
- Entering or re-entering the field of play without the referee's permission
- Deliberately leaving the field of play without the referee's permission

Red cards are used to send a player off the field, and can be issued for the following offenses:

- Serious foul play
- Violent conduct
- Spitting at an opponent or any other person
- Denying the opposing team a goal or an obvious goal-scoring opportunity by deliberately handling the ball (the goalkeeper being an exception)
- Denying an obvious goal-scoring opportunity to an opponent moving towards the player's goal by an offense punishable by a free kick or a penalty kick
- Using offensive or abusive language and/or gestures

- Receiving a second caution (yellow card) in the same match

What Parents Really Need to Know

The referee is always correct, and he/she will NOT change their call if you yell. In fact, the more you yell, the less chance you have of getting a favorable call on the next play. Every time you yell, you decrease the odds of getting a favorable call by 5%. (I just made up the last sentence, but I wish I could make that one a law.)

A Few Items to Clarify

1. Just because a player falls down does not mean it is a foul. The person just may have fallen, it happens.

2. There is no exemption because you "got all ball." A foul is a foul whether you hit 5% of the ball or all the ball.

3. A ball that is kicked and hits a player's hand or arm is not automatically a hand ball.

4. A ball that is kicked and hits a player's hand or arm is not automatically a hand ball. (I wrote it twice, so you would not think this was a misprint.)

5. Ball to hand = No hand ball

   Hand to ball = hand ball

6. It is the judgement of the referee to determine if the hand ball was accidental or an attempt to gain an advantage. The referee will typically be 5 to 10 yards away from the play and a parent will be 100 to 1,000 yards away; who would you believe?

7. If two players are going shoulder to shoulder and one falls down, this is called being clumsy, not a foul.

Bumping or playing physical is not a foul until the arms or elbows go up.

8. Keepers are like quarterbacks in the NFL, they are a protected species, stay away.

9. A ball kicked back to a keeper cannot be handled by the player or it is an infraction.

10. Basically, a player cannot kick, trip, jump at, charge, strike, push, hold, or spit at an opponent.

11. If the foul is serious, it is a yellow card. If the foul is dangerous, it is a red card.

12. I am not sure if I mentioned this or not, but the referee will typically be 5 to 10 yards away from the play and a parent will be 100 to 1,000 yards away; who would you believe?

13. The referee is always correct and if the referee is me, I am not only always correct, but the call is brilliant.

Law 13: Free Kicks

IFAB rule: Free Kick is broken into two categories, direct and indirect. A direct kick can be shot directly into the opponent's goal without touching another player. An indirect free kick is indicated by the referee raising his hand during the kick. An indirect kick can only go into the goal if it has subsequently been touched by another player first. The ball must be stationary for both types of kicks.

What Parents Really Need to Know

For both a direct and indirect kick, the opposing player must be 10 yards away. The reason that some referees have a spray can is to designate the 10 yards. This is done because some "clever" players try to inch closer to the ball after the referee turns her back. Generally, a direct kick is caused by a foul or hand ball and everything else is indirect, like offside or dangerous play. Many youth leagues will not allow direct kicks until after U-8.

Law 14: The Penalty Kick

IFAB rule: A penalty kick is awarded either when a defensive player fouls an attacking player or commits a handball in his/her team's penalty area. The penalty kick is placed at the penalty spot, and all players on both teams must remain outside the penalty box during the shot. They may enter the box immediately after the shot is taken. The goalkeeper may move horizontally along the goal line before the shot is taken, but he may not come off the line until the ball is struck.

What Parents Really Need to Know

A penalty kick occurs when a foul or handball is committed in the penalty area by the defending team. To be perfectly honest, too many referees are tentative when calling a PK. One person takes the PK from a spot 12 yards in front of the center of the goal while everyone else must be outside the penalty area. Listed below is a figure of possible outcomes for a penalty kick.

Table 1: Penalty Kick Scenarios

	Outcome of Penalty Kick	
	Goal	**No Goal**
Encroachment by attacking player	Penalty is retaken	Indirect free kick
Encroachment by defending player	Goal	Penalty is retaken
Offense by goalkeeper	Goal	Penalty is retaken and caution for goalkeeper
Ball kicked backwards	Indirect free kick	Indirect free kick
Illegal feinting	Indirect free kick and caution for kicker	Indirect free kick and caution for kicker
Wrong kicker	Indirect free kick and caution for wrong kicker	Indirect free kick and caution for wrong kicker

These are just a few of the scenarios that referees must not only know but be able to make split second decisions on. So, the next time you think about yelling at a referee, stop and think a little more.

PKs are also a standard way to determine the winner after both teams tie in regulation and stay tied after the overtime periods. Each team can pick five players from the participants who are on the field at the end of the game. Each team takes turns kicking the penalty team kick until one team wins.

One of the most bizarre situations occurred in the 2009/10 season in an Argentinian league. Two teams were playing in the qualifying round of the Apertura for the Ronda Final at the end of the season. I don't know about you, but I do not miss the Apertura for the Ronda Final for anything. With the match tied at 3-3, the teams headed to the shootout. Each team takes five penalty kicks to declare a winner, but if by some chance the score is still tied, the teams keep kicking until one team scores and the other team misses. In the highest score ever officially recorded, the final tally was 21-20. To add to the phenomena, only one penalty kick was missed, with 40 attempts made by the players.

Law 15: The Throw-In

IFAB rule: A throw-in is awarded when the possessing team plays the ball out of bounds over the touchline. While taking a throw-in, a player must release the ball with both hands simultaneously and keep both feet firmly planted on the ground. If these conditions are not met, play is stopped and the throw-in is given to the opposing team. Players are not allowed to score directly off a throw-in.

What Parents Really Need to Know

When girls are playing soccer and the ball goes out, one player from the team getting the throw-in will run after the ball. When boys are playing and the ball goes out, at least one player from each team runs after the ball in an attempt to persuade the referee that they get the throw-in. Here is another difference between the sexes. When a boy gets fouled, watch him for at least two minutes, because he will retaliate. When a girl gets fouled, you have to watch her for four weeks because revenge is best served cold.

The two most important rules on a throw-in are: 1) both feet must be on the ground and 2) the ball must be thrown with both hands over the head. Parents please note that the player can hop, skip, jump, or do the tango so long as these two rules are followed. Throwing the ball directly into the ground six inches in front of you is legal. It is silly, but it is legal. I hear parents complain all the time that if the ball spins or moves in an unusual fashion, it is a bad throw in. Sorry, but as long as both hands are over the head and not on the side, this is legal.

What players typically try to do is push the envelope by taking a running start on the throw-in to get an extra 5-10 yards down the field. A good referee will make the person throw it in again. Some players also attempt a flip when they throw in the ball, but most people believe this is pure showmanship. Throw ins are a vital part of a match. Typically, there are 40 to 50 per game and they constitute about 12 minutes of play, which is about 13% of the match, which is similar to special teams play in American football. Liverpool actually has a "Throw in Coach," which has garnered some criticism. Nevertheless, this is my new career aspiration.

Law 16: The Goal Kick

IFAB rule: A goal kick is awarded when the offensive team plays the ball out of bounds over the defensive team's goal line. After the ball is out of play, the defender or goalkeeper may place the ball anywhere within the six-yard goal box and kick the ball back into play.

What Parents Really Need to Know

Telling your son or daughter to place the ball for a goal kick and then pick it up to run to the other side of the penalty box only to kick it from a different location not only fools no one, but it is illegal.

Why did the soccer ball quit the team?

He was tired of being kicked around.

Where do soccer players go to dance?

A soccer ball.

What lights up a soccer stadium?

A soccer match.

Law 17: The Corner Kick

IFAB rule: A corner kick is awarded to the offensive team when the defensive team plays the ball out of bounds over its goal line. The ball is placed within the corner area and is kicked back into play by the offensive team. Players can score directly off a corner kick.

What Parents Really Need to Know

A corner kick, or goal kick, is taken when the ball leaves the field across a goal line—you know, either end of the field with a goal. If the offensive team kicks it out, play is restarted with a goal kick. If the defensive team kicks it out, play is restarted with a corner kick.

Here is a play that almost every youth soccer team has tried, which most parents do not understand. Team A has a corner kick and A1 moves to take the shot. He gets ready, but then motions for A2 to take the shot, but before he leaves the corner, he touches the ball, which moves one or two inches. A2 runs over to supposedly take the kick, and then because it really is a live ball, dribbles toward the goal to take a shot. This is totally legal, however, if before he leaves the corner, A1 yells to A2, "Hey you come and take the shot," this is deception and not legal.

Here is a fun fact about corner kicks. A team cannot score an own goal on a corner kick. Think about this one. If a team is taking a corner kick, the player would have to mistakenly kick the ball the entire length of the pitch and score against his own keeper some 110 yards away. I seriously doubt this has ever happened, and if it has, the player should be rewarded somehow, that is one heck of a kick.

Responsibilities of The Referee

- Enforces the Laws of the Game.

- Controls the match in cooperation with the assistant referees.

- Stops, suspends, or abandons the match, at his discretion, for any infringements of the Laws.

- Allows play to continue until the ball is out of play if a player is, in his opinion, only slightly injured. This means that if the referee believes the player is faking an injury, she can keep the game going. Of course, a soccer player would never exaggerate or fake an injury. Never.

- Punishes the more serious offense when a player commits more than one offense at the same time

- Takes action against team officials who fail to conduct themselves in a responsible manner and may, at his discretion, expel them from the field of play and its immediate surroundings

- Acts on the advice of the assistant referees regarding incidents that he has not seen.

- Provides the appropriate authorities with a match report, which includes information on any disciplinary action taken against players and/or team officials and any other incidents that occurred before, during or after the match.

- The referee is always correct, even when he is wrong.

Final Recommendations

Parents, overreacting at a youth soccer game is embarrassing, just stop it. But let's be honest, this is a complex problem. Here are the recommended steps for addressing the situation.

1. It might actually be a good idea to have a penalty box for parents. Hockey uses a penalty box successfully, and in soccer, the ref could simply put a parent in a "box" for five or ten minutes as needed.

2. Soccer leagues need to educate parents. Don't just assume that parents know the game of soccer and understand the negative consequences of pretending to be the coach. Talk with parents, conduct classes, and educate them on proper behavior.

3. The Matheny Manifesto is not a bad idea, but at the very least parents and coaches should sign an agreement. Coaches need to communicate to players and parents, provide feedback to players, and serve as role models. They cannot be yelling at players and then expect parents to do the opposite. Parents need to be parents and not coaches. Be involved with the game but work with coaches as a team. And for goodness sake, do not yell at a ten-year old referee. Pretend she is your daughter and abide by common sense.

4. Parents need to police one another (no pun intended). There is a level of accountability for the group of parents to add support to their children and the game.

5. Coaches should enforce the following three rules: a) players need honest and timely feedback to improve; b) talk to the player, not the parent, this helps the child with independence as they learn to advocate for themselves, c) utilize a 24 hour rule, no parent can call the coach within 24 hours of the game.

6. The United States might need to follow the lead of Norway, which has a unique youth-sports policy based on equality. Norway values participation and all of the associated benefits over winning. Any

youth club with athletes less than 13 years of age cannot publish scores of events. American youth soccer needs to tone down the emphasis on winning, traveling teams, winning, trophies, and winning. But that will not make parents happy.

7. No child ever works hard to be a failure, and no parent ever had a child that was a failure; just ask them.

8. At no point should a parent ever say anything to a referee or opposing player except maybe, "Nice job."

9. Everyone needs to learn the laws of soccer.

10. Above everything else, realize that it is only a game and there are more important issues to address than a U-7 soccer match. Let the kids play and fail and succeed. Remember, Walt Disney was fired from the Kansas City Star purportedly because his editor felt he "lacked imagination." Bob Dylan's band, the Golden Chords, lost a high-school talent competition to a tap dancing act. The point here is that coaches need to treat everyone as an individual and parents need to understand people need to fail. If it is not obvious by now, the key to being a parent is, being a parent and not a coach, referee, or felon. Learn what it is to be a servant leader and help your kids become servant leaders on and off the pitch. When it comes to the soccer matches, it is easy. Simply say, "I love you," and, "Did you have fun?"

11. Parents should buy a nice van for all the soccer matches and then stay in it during the games.

Closing Thought

Amanda Visek, an exercise science professor at Milken Institute School of Public Health (Milken Institute SPH) at the George Washington University conducted a study in 2014 asking 142 soccer players, 37 coaches, and 57 parents to identify what makes soccer fun. The researchers analyzed the data to find 81 specific items. At the top of the list were the following: Being a good sport, Trying hard, Positive coaching, Learning and improving, Game time support, Games, Practices, Team friendships, Mental bonuses, Team rituals, and Swag. At the bottom of the list, surprising to parents, was Winning, followed by playing in tournaments, cool uniforms, and expensive equipment. Kids get it. They understand why it is fun to play sports. Now we just need to convince the parents (Fackelmann, 2014).

References

A Mom From the Losing Team. (2017). http://www.huffingtonpost.com/lindsay-ferrier/notes-from-the-losing-team_b_5939548.html?utm_hp_ref=tw

At Your Own Risk. (2018). "The Benefits of High School and Youth Sports." https://www.atyourownrisk.org/benefits-of-sports/

Avalos, Gilma. (2013). Youth Soccer Tournament at Disney Turns Violent. https://www.nbcmiami.com/news/local/Youth-Soccer-Tournament-at-Disney-Turns-Violent-216518621.html

Berlin, Jeremy. (February 2013). Joy Is Round. *National Geographic* magazine. http://www.nationalgeographic.com/magazine/2013/02/soccer-joy/

Brentwood Soccer Club. http://www.brentwoodsoccerclub.com/girlsteams/clash/192142.html?cv=1

Coughlin, Paul. (2008). Helicopter Moms, Momma Bears, and Grizzly Moms. http://www.crosswalk.com/blogs/PCoughlin/11576385/

Covey, Stephen. (2004). *The 7 Habits of Highly Effective People.* New York: Simon and Schuster.

Deresiewicz, William. (2015). *Excellent Sheep: The Miseducation of the American Elite and the Way to a Meaningful Life.* New York: Free Press.

Ericsson, Anders, & Pool, Robert. (April 5, 2016). *Peak: Secrets from the New Science of Expertise.* Eamon Dolan/Houghton Mifflin Harcourt.

Fackelmann, Kathy. (July 10, 2014). Being a Good Sport Ranks as the Top "Fun" Factor in Study of Youth Sports. https://publichealth.gwu.edu/content/being-good-sport-ranks-top-%E2%80%9Cfun%E2%80%9D-factor-study-youth-sports

Frank's Case Book. (2002). The Role of a Soccer Referee, http://s171185354.onlinehome.us/2002/09/22/the-role-of-a-soccer-referee/

Froh, Tim. (April 16, 2018). "'My under-10 matches are the worst': No end in sight to youth referee abuse." https://www.theguardian.com/sport/2018/apr/16/my-under-10-matches-are-the-worst-no-end-in-sight-to-youth-referee-abuse

Gladwell, Malcom. (2008). *Outliers: The Story of Success.* Columbus Georgia: Little, Brown and Company.

Gruner, Charles. (1997). *The game of humor.* New Bruswick, NJ: Transaction.

Harmon, Gary. (May 29, 2008). Soccer mom gets red card. https://www.gjsentinel.com/hp/content/news/stories/2008/05/29/053008_1a_soccer.html?imw=Y

Hessler Jr., Carl. (Jun 24, 2008). Soccer Mom Heads To Court On Theft Charges. *https://www.pottsmerc.com/news/soccer-mom-waives-theft-charges/article_fefa5c3f-0bc6-5e77-972a-6f6625488e9c.html*

Kohn, Alfie. (1994), The Risks of Rewards. https://www.alfiekohn.org/article/risks-rewards/

Kyonka, Nick. (2007). Irate Soccer Mom Brings Game to Screeching Halt. *The Star.* https://www.thestar.com/

news/gta/2007/07/24/irate_soccer_mom_brings_game_to_screeching_halt.html

Madden, Paul. (no date). Offside Rule Explained for Women. https://www.bone.me.uk/offside-rule.php. Disclaimer: Use at your own risk. Don't take any of this site seriously, it's not advice, nor is it a manual.

Manalapan Soccer Club. (2014). "When Parent Misbehave -- Send Them to Bootcamp." http://manalapansoccer.demosphere.com/TrainingInformation/145101.html

Manchester Evening News. (2007). Parents use mobiles to foil penalties. https://www.manchestereveningnews.co.uk/news/greater-manchester-news/parents-use-mobiles-to-foil-penalties-979484?cv=1

Matheny, Mike. (2009). *The Matheny Manifesto*. https://www.mikematheny.com/sites/default/files/docs/MathenyManifesto.pdf

Mattison, Andy. (2000). Sports Rage: Why Are Parents Out of Control? *Neirad. 63*(3). http://neirad.darienps.net/print/november2000.pdf

Mehrabian, A. (1971). *Silent messages*. Belmont, CA: Wadsworth.

Mendoza, Robert. (no date). Soccer is a Joke. "Coaching CHILDREN." http://www.fundamentalsoccer.com/RMendoza.html

NAIA website. (no date). Student-Athlete Pledge. http://www.naia.org/fls/27900/1NAIA/championsofcharacter/NAIAChampionsofCharacter_StudentAthletePledge.pdf?DB_OEM_ID=27900

National Athletic Trainers' Association (2018). The Benefits of High School and Youth Sports. https://www.atyourownrisk.org/benefits-of-sports/

New York Times. (Dec. 25, 1996). Player, Father Admit Sharpening Buckle. https://www.nytimes.com/1996/12/25/sports/player-father-admit-sharpening-buckle.html

Offside. (no date). Facebook page. https://www.facebook.com/youreoffside/

Omega Athletic Club. (2007). http://omegasc.com/default.asp?message=7

Reyna, Claudio. (2008). http://manageyourleague.com/LDS/site/uploaded_files/Coaches%20Corner/Quotes.pdf

Rockwood Preparatory Academy web page, n.d., http://rockwoodprep.org/servant-leadership/

Ryan, Richard, & Deci, Edward. (2000). Self-determination theory and the facilitation of intrinsic motivation, social development, and well-being. *American Psychologist*, 55, 68-78. https://dx.doi.org/10.1037/0003-066X.55.1.68

Seibel, Jacqui. (2008). Off-duty cop, other dad spar at soccer game. *http://www.jsonline.com/story/index.aspx?id=763785*

Simmons, Joanna. (2007). A Soccer Folly. Ezine articles. http://ezinearticles.com/?A-Soccer-Folly&id=517919

Soccer Moms from Hell. (June 22, 2008). http://www.momlogic.com/2008/06/little_league_drama.php

Spears, Larry C. (1995). *Reflections on leadership: How Robert K. Greenleaf's Servant Leadership influenced today's top management* thinkers. New York: Wiley Press.

Spencer, Peter. (Feb. 2007). Parents Use Mobiles to Foil Penalties. http://www.manchestereveningnews.co.uk/news/s/233/233995_parents_use_mobiles_to_foil_penalties.html

Stella Maddox tweet. (May 25, 2015). https://twitter.com/StellaGMaddox/status/602991321184399362?ref_src=twsrc%5Etfw%7Ctwcamp%5Etweetembed%7Ctwterm%5E602991321184399362&ref_url=https%3A%2F%2Fwww.huffingtonpost.com%2Fentry%2Ftweets-parents-kids-sports_us_5acb799ee4b07a3485e6c204

Stiles, Judith. (Nov. 2005). Soccer dad is arrested for assault at Pier 40. *The Villager.* 75(27). http://thevillager.com/villager_134/soccerdadisarrested.html

The Fatref blogpost. (2007). http://refwrites.blogspot.com/2007/07/norwegian-mum-goes-nuts-on-football.html

Thompson, Derek. (Nov. 6, 2018). American Meritocracy Is Killing Youth Sports. The Atlantic. https://www.theatlantic.com/ideas/archive/2018/11/income-inequality-explains-decline-youth-sports/574975/

TOP 10 Tips for Coaching Your Child's Team (According to Kids). (no date). *Sports Illustrated for Kids.* http://bgparks.org/pdf/youth-sports/soccer/Ten%20Tips%20To%20Coaching%20Your%20Childs%20Team.pdf

U.S. Soccer Federation. (2014). Our Game. Our Stories. http://togetherwearsoccer.org/our-game-our-stories-zohn

Umpires and Referees Stopping Assaults Forever. (no date). https://ur-safe.org/

Urban dictionary. (2005). https://www.urbandictionary.com/define.php?term=Passive-Aggressive

West Chester United SC. (2008). You know you are a soccer family when... http://www.wcusc.org/Travel/97B1/269626.html

Woitalla, Mike. (2007). "Time for a Children's Revolt." *Youth Insider*. http://www.youthsoccerfun.com/2007/05/time_for_a_childrens_revolt.html

Wong, Edward. (May 6, 2001). New Rules for Soccer Parents: 1) No Yelling. 2) No Hitting Refs." *New York Times*, 1, 30.

Words of Advice for Soccer Parents. (2011). Blog. http://www.reyes-chow.com/2011/09/advice-for-soccer-parents/

Select MSI Books

Self-Help Books

A Woman's Guide to Self-Nurturing (Romer)

Care for the Catholic Caregiver (Franklin)

Creative Aging: A Baby Boomer's Guide to Successful Living (Vassiliadis & Romer)

Divorced! Survival Techniques for Singles over Forty (Romer)

How to Get Happy and Stay That Way: Practical Techniques for Putting Joy into Your Life (Romer)

How to Live from Your Heart (Hucknall) (Book of the Year Finalist)

Living Well with Chronic Illness (Charnas)

Overcoming the Odds (C. Leaver)

Publishing for Smarties: Finding a Publisher (Ham)

Recovering from Domestic Violence, Abuse, and Stalking (Romer)

Survival of the Caregiver (Snyder)

The Rose and the Sword: How to Balance Your Feminine and Masculine Energies (Bach & Hucknall)

The Widower's Guide to a New Life (Romer)(Book of the Year Finalist)

Widow: A Survival Guide for the First Year (Romer)

Widow: How to Survive (and Thrive!) in Your 2d, 3d, and 4th Years (Romer)

Inspirational and Religious Books

A Believer-in-Waiting's First Encounters with God (Mahlou)

A Guide to Bliss: Transforming Your Life through Mind Expansion (Tubali)

Christmas at the Mission: A Cat's View of Catholic Beliefs and Customs (Sula)

El Poder de lo Transpersonal (Ustman)

Everybody's Little Book of Everyday Prayers (MacGregor)

Joshuanism (Tosto)

Living in Blue Sky Mind: Basic Buddhist Teachings for a Happy Life (Diedrichs)

Passing On: How to Prepare Ourselves for the Afterlife (Romer)

Puertas a la Eternidad (Ustman)

Surviving Cancer, Healing People: One Cat's Story (Sula)

Tale of a Mission Cat (Sula)

The Seven Wisdoms of Life: A Journey into the Chakras (Tubali) (Book of the Year Finalist)

When You're Shoved from the Right, Look to Your Left: Metaphors of Islamic Humanism (O. Imady)

MEMOIRS

57 Steps to Paradise: Finding Love in Midlife and Beyond (Lorenz)

Blest Atheist (Mahlou)

Forget the Goal, the Journey Counts . . . 71 Jobs Later (Stites)

From Deep Within: A Forensic and Clinical Psychologist's Journey (Lewis)

Good Blood: A Journey of Healing (Schaffer)

Healing from Incest: Intimate Conversations with My Therapist (Henderson & Emerton) (Book of the Year Finalist)

It Only Hurts When I Can't Run: One Girl's Story (Parker)

Las Historias de Mi Vida (Ustman)

Of God, Rattlesnakes, and Okra (Easterling)

Road to Damascus (E. Imady)

The Optimistic Food Addict (Fisanick)

Tucker and Me (Harvey)

FOREIGN CULTURE

Syrian Folktales (M. Imady)

The Rise and Fall of Muslim Civil Society (O. Imady)

The Subversive Utopia: Louis Kahn and the Question of National Jewish Style in Jerusalem (Sakr)

Thoughts without a Title (Henderson)

Psychology & Philosophy

Anger Anonymous: The Big Book on Anger Addiction (Ortman)

Anxiety Anonymous: The Big Book on Anxiety Addiction (Ortman)

Awesome Couple Communication: Expressing What You Mean and Understanding What the Other Meant (Pickett)

Depression Anonymous: The Big Book on Depression Addiction (Ortman)

From Deep Within (Lewis)

Road Map to Power (Husain & Husain)

The Marriage Whisperer: How to Improve Your Relationship Overnight (Pickett) (IPPY Living Now Gold Medal)

Understanding the Analyst: Socionics in Everyday Life (Quinelle)

Understanding the Challenge of "No" for Children with Autism (McNeil)

Understanding the Critic: Socionics in Everyday Life (Quinelle)

Understanding the Entrepreneur: Socionics in Everyday Life (Quinelle)

Understanding the People around You: An Introduction to Socionics (Filatova)

Understanding the Seeker: Socionics in Everyday Life (Quinelle)

Humor

How My Cat Made Me a Better Man (Feig) (Book of the Year Finalist)

Mommy Poisoned Our House Guest (S. Leaver)

The Musings of a Carolina Yankee (Amidon)

Parenting

365 Teacher Secrets for Parents: Fun Ways to Help Your Child in Elementary School (McKinley & Trombly) [Recommended by US Review of Books; Selected as USA Best Book Finalist]

Courageous Parents (Omer)

How to Be a Good Mommy When You're Sick (Graves)

Lessons of Labor (Aziz)